IMMIGRANTS
WHO RETURNED HOME

The Peoples of North America

IMMIGRANTS
WHO RETURNED HOME

Betty Boyd Caroli

CHELSEA HOUSE PUBLISHERS

New York   Philadelphia

On the cover: Ricki Rosen, an American who emigrated to Israel, at a Fourth of July picnic in Jerusalem.

CHELSEA HOUSE PUBLISHERS
Editor-in-Chief: Nancy Toff
Executive Editor: Remmel T. Nunn
Managing Editor: Karyn Gullen Browne
Copy Chief: Juliann Barbato
Picture Editor: Adrian G. Allen
Art Director: Maria Epes
Manufacturing Manager: Gerald Levine
Systems Manager: Rachel Vigier

The Peoples of North America
Senior Editor: Sean Dolan

Staff for IMMIGRANTS WHO RETURNED HOME
Copy Editor: Philip Koslow
Deputy Copy Chief: Nicole Bowen
Editorial Assistant: Elizabeth Nix
Picture Research: PAR/NYC
Assistant Art Director: Loraine Machlin
Senior Designer: Noreen M. Lamb
Production Manager: Joseph Romano
Production Coordinator: Marie Claire Cebrián
Cover Illustration: Paul Biniasz
Banner Design: Hrana Janto

Library of Congress Cataloging-in-Publication Data
Caroli, Betty Boyd
  Immigrants Who Returned Home.
    (Peoples of North America)
  Includes bibliographical references.
  Summary: Examines the motivations of immigrants from Ireland, Sweden, Asia, and other parts of the world who return to their homelands for political, cultural, economic, and other reasons.
    1. Return migration—Juvenile literature.
2. Immigrants—North America—Juvenile literature.
3. North America—Emigration and immigration—Juvenile literature. [1. Return migration. 2. North America—Emigration and immigration] I. Title. II. Series.
JV6217.37 1990
3041.8 89-24006
ISBN 0-87754-864-1
      0-7910-0296-9 (pbk.)

CONTENTS

THE PEOPLES OF NORTH AMERICA

CHELSEA HOUSE PUBLISHERS

A NATION OF NATIONS

Daniel Patrick Moynihan

The Constitution of the United States begins: "We the People of the United States . . . " Yet, as we know, the United States is not made up of a single group of people. It is made up of many peoples. Immigrants from Europe, Asia, Africa, and Central and South America settled in North America seeking a new life filled with opportunities unavailable in their homeland. Coming from many nations, they forged one nation and made it their own. More than 100 years ago, Walt Whitman expressed this perception of America as a melting pot: "Here is not merely a nation, but a teeming Nation of nations."

Although the ingenuity and acts of courage of these immigrants, our ancestors, shaped the North American way of life, we sometimes take their contributions for granted. This fine series, *The Peoples of North America*, examines the experiences and contributions of the immigrants and how these contributions determined the future of the United States and Canada.

Immigrants did not abandon their ethnic traditions when they reached the shores of North America. Each ethnic group had its own customs and traditions, and each brought different experiences, accomplishments, skills, values, styles of dress, and tastes in food that lingered long after its arrival. Yet this profusion of differences created a singularity, or bond, among the immigrants.

The United States and Canada are unusual in this respect. Whereas religious and ethnic differences have sparked intolerance throughout the rest of the world—from the 17th-century religious wars to the 19th-century nationalist movements in Europe to the near extermination of the Jewish people under Nazi Germany—North Americans have struggled to learn how to respect each other's differences and live in harmony.

Millions of immigrants from scores of homelands brought diversity to our continent. In a mass migration, some 12 million immigrants passed through the waiting rooms of New York's Ellis Island; thousands more came to the West Coast. At first, these immigrants were welcomed because labor was needed to meet the demands of the Industrial Age. Soon, however, the new immigrants faced the prejudice of earlier immigrants who saw them as a burden on the economy. Legislation was passed to limit immigration. The Chinese Exclusion Act of 1882 was among the first laws closing the doors to the promise of America. The Japanese were also effectively excluded by this law. In 1924, Congress set immigration quotas on a country-by-country basis.

Such prejudices might have triggered war, as they did in Europe, but North Americans chose negotiation and compromise instead. This determination to resolve differences peacefully has been the hallmark of the peoples of North America.

The remarkable ability of Americans to live together as one people was seriously threatened by the issue of slavery. It was a symptom of growing intolerance in the world. Thousands of settlers from the British Isles had arrived in the colonies as indentured servants, agreeing to work for a specified number of years on farms or as apprentices in return for passage to America and room and board. When the first Africans arrived in the then-British colonies during the 17th century, some colonists thought that they too should be treated as indentured servants. Eventually, the question of whether the Africans should be viewed as indentured, like the English, or as slaves who could be owned for life, was considered in a Maryland court. The court's calamitous decree held that blacks were slaves bound to lifelong servitude, and so were their children. America went through a time of moral examination and civil war before it finally freed African slaves and their descendants. The principle that all people are created equal had faced its greatest challenge and survived.

Yet the court ruling that set blacks apart from other races fanned flames of discrimination that burned long after slavery was abolished—and that still flicker today. The concept of racism had existed for centuries in countries throughout the world. For instance, when the Manchus conquered China in the 13th century, they decreed that Chinese and Manchus could not intermarry. To impress their superiority on the conquered Chinese, the Manchus ordered all Chinese men to wear their hair in a long braid called a queue.

By the 19th century, some intellectuals took up the banner of racism, citing Charles Darwin. Darwin's scientific studies hypothesized that highly evolved animals were dominant over other animals. Some advocates of this theory applied it to humans, asserting that certain races were more highly evolved than others and thus were superior.

This philosophy served as the basis for a new form of discrimination, not only against nonwhite people but also against various ethnic groups. Asians faced harsh discrimination and were depicted by popular 19th-century newspaper cartoonists as depraved, degenerate, and deficient in intelligence. When the Irish flooded American cities to escape the famine in Ireland, the cartoonists caricatured the typical "Paddy" (a common term for Irish immigrants) as an apelike creature with jutting jaw and sloping forehead.

By the 20th century, racism and ethnic prejudice had given rise to virulent theories of a Northern European master race. When Adolf Hitler came to power in Germany in 1933, he popularized the notion of Aryan supremacy. *Aryan*, a term referring to the Indo-European races, was applied to so-called superior physical characteristics such as blond hair, blue eyes, and delicate facial features. Anyone with darker and heavier features was considered inferior. Buttressed by these theories, the German Nazi state from 1933 to 1945 set out to destroy European Jews, along with Poles, Russians, and other groups considered inferior. It nearly succeeded. Millions of these people were exterminated.

The tragedies brought on by ethnic and racial intolerance throughout the world demonstrate the importance of North America's efforts to create a society free of prejudice and inequality.

A relatively recent example of the New World's desire to resolve ethnic friction nonviolently is the solution the Canadians found to a conflict between two ethnic groups. A long-standing dispute as to whether Canadian culture was properly English or French resurfaced in the mid-1960s, dividing the peoples of the French-speaking Quebec Province from those of the English-speaking provinces. Relations grew tense, then bitter, then violent. The Royal Commission on Bilingualism and Biculturalism was established to study the growing crisis and to propose measures to ease the tensions. As a result of the commission's recommendations, all official documents and statements from the national government's capital at Ottawa are now issued in both French and English, and bilingual education is encouraged.

The year 1980 marked a coming of age for the United States's ethnic heritage. For the first time, the U.S. Census asked people about their ethnic background. Americans chose from more than 100 groups, including French Basque, Spanish Basque, French Canadian, Afro-American, Peruvian, Armenian, Chinese, and Japanese. The ethnic group with the largest response was English (49.6 million). More than 100 million Americans claimed ancestors from the British Isles, which includes England, Ireland, Wales, and Scotland. There were almost as many Germans (49.2 million) as English. The Irish-American population (40.2 million) was third, but the next largest ethnic group, the Afro-Americans, was a distant fourth (21 million). There was a sizable group of French ancestry (13 million), as well as of Italian (12 million). Poles, Dutch, Swedes, Norwegians, and Russians followed. These groups, and other smaller ones, represent the wondrous profusion of ethnic influences in North America.

Canada, too, has learned more about the diversity of its population. Studies conducted during the French/English conflict showed that Canadians were descended from Ukrainians, Germans, Italians, Chinese, Japanese, native Indians, and Eskimos, among others.

Canada found it had no ethnic majority, although nearly half of its immigrant population had come from the British Isles. Canada, like the United States, is a land of immigrants for whom mutual tolerance is a matter of reason as well as principle.

The people of North America are the descendants of one of the greatest migrations in history. And that migration is not over. Koreans, Vietnamese, Nicaraguans, Cubans, and many others are heading for the shores of North America in large numbers. This mix of cultures shapes every aspect of our lives. To understand ourselves, we must know something about our diverse ethnic ancestry. Nothing so defines the North American nations as the motto on the Great Seal of the United States: *E Pluribus Unum*—Out of Many, One.

A TWO-WAY STREET

The story of immigration—of the millions of Europeans, Asians, and Africans who have come to these shores seeking fulfillment of the promise of equality and justice symbolized by the Statue of Liberty in New York harbor—has become a familiar part of the American saga. But of all the words written and spoken about the immigrants, how many have been devoted to those who returned home? Yet among the millions who came to North America and found some degree of satisfaction—if not always fame and fortune—were millions of others who came and left. Some were disillusioned; others had never meant to stay. Some remained only a few months; others spent nearly a lifetime. Whatever their reason for leaving, the returnees form an important part of the immigration record because they had a double effect. In coming to America they brought their traditions with them; in leaving they carried new ideas back to their homelands. And that question—to remain or to return home—is at the very heart of the immigrant experience, concerned as it is with the very same issues—patriotism, loyalty, family, quality of life, freedom—that make the decision to emigrate such a complex one.

In one sense the obscurity of the repatriates is not surprising. Because for more than a century the single word *America* has been a synonym for adventure and success for so many, few were willing to admit to having met with disappointment in the New World. For most immigrants, the trip to America was long, undertaken only at great cost and considerable risk. For the returnees, to criticize America was tantamount to announcing one's error and admitting to failure.

But it was this glittering image of America as the Promised Land that made it difficult for it to fulfill the expectations of all those who succumbed to its allure. Early discoverers, such as Christopher Columbus and Giovanni da Verrazano, exaggerated the amount of gold to be found and the hospitality of the native people. Although America's natural wealth and vast expanses of seemingly unclaimed land were unmatched by any of the countries of Europe, no one could have prepared the earliest settlers for the harshness of North American winters and the difficulties of starting life anew thousands of miles from family and friends. Glowing reports of immediate wealth and gentle reception led potential settlers to anticipate far more than they could possibly achieve. When reality set in, in the form of disease, attacks from hostile Indians, or the need to clear forests for farmland, many men and women cast a longing eye toward home.

From the days of its first settlement, America seemed to offer newcomers that rarest of commodities, freedom—be it to practice an unpopular religion, obtain an education, or seek economic advancement unconstrained by class or legal restraints. (The same was not true, of course, for the earliest inhabitants of the land, the Indians, nor for the black Africans who arrived on these shores in chains to be auctioned off as slave labor for the

The Frenchman Alexis de Tocqueville was the most famous of the Europeans who visited the United States to report on American life. His famous Democracy in America, *published in 1835, remains the most penetrating study of America's experiment with representative government.*

ambitious settlers.) With so much unsettled land, it seemed likely that North America could offer a haven to all, but immigrants found this too to be a chimera, like the gold with which American streets were said to be paved. Some of those who fled to the New World in order to freely practice their religion, such as the Puritans, who were among the earliest settlers of New England, were unwilling to grant other settlers the same tolerance they sought. Blacks were generally welcome only as slaves, and in the 19th century the huge numbers of Catholic immigrants who came to the United States found themselves the victims of virulent prejudice by the Protestant majority. Today, hundreds of thousands of Central Americans, fleeing poverty and political oppression, risk their lives to reach the United States, only to be denied legal entry; should they enter illegally, they are often relegated to a life of poverty and exploitation. Indeed, each new group of immigrants has generally been viewed with mistrust by more established

A 19th-century advertisement by the American Emigrant Company, a labor agency, offers to provide employers with immigrant laborers. During the two great waves of immigration to the United States (1840–80; 1880–1914), the need of American industrialists for manpower coincided with the desire of much of Europe's lower and middle classes to come to America.

Americans. While many persevered, overcoming discrimination as well as numerous other obstacles to success in their adopted country, many others returned home. Political events involving the nations of their forebears motivated many to return. For example, British settlers and their descendants left the former colonies for the Old World after the newly formed United States prevailed over Britain in the revolutionary war; some of the French settlers of New France returned to Europe following France's defeat by Great Britain in the Seven Years' War, which gave Britain control of Canada. Many Jews, driven to America by centuries of anti-Semitism, headed for the Jewish homeland of Israel in the decades following its attainment of independence in 1948. Some of today's Central American immigrants have expressed hope that an end to the political violence that has rent their nations in recent decades will allow them to return home.

Many of those who returned home had never intended to stay. Commitment to remain in America was never required for entry, and some people made the journey solely for adventure. They came to trace a river to its source, catalog unfamiliar plants, or observe the ways of the Indians. Particularly in the late 18th and early 19th centuries, many Europeans came to study the United States's noble experiment in representative government or to examine an odious facet of American life, the peculiar institution of slavery. As the advent of the steamship made transoceanic travel cheaper and faster, hundreds of thousands of men journeyed to the United States in search of work. Never meaning to stay permanently, they left their wives and children in the homeland and looked for work building the subways of New York and the railroads of the West, or mining coal in the anthracite fields of western Pennsylvania, or working in factories or mills in the industrial cities of the Northeast. Aware that in the United States and Canada they could earn several times what they had earned in the old country, they planned to stay only until they had

Immigrant laborers at work at the McCormick factory in Chicago, which produced farm equipment. Although many immigrants worked long hours doing dangerous and dirty work, most viewed life in America as an opportunity for significant economic advancement. Many hoped to return home with money they had saved in America.

put away enough money to buy property or a business at home. A returned Italian workman explained the New World's attraction for these immigrants quite succinctly: "There was always bread in America."

Although the United States has long since closed the door it once held open for the world's tired and poor, it remains the land of opportunity to many who are willing to leave behind family, friends, and country for the better life that they believe awaits them in America. For today's immigrants, whether impoverished farm workers from Mexico, political and economic refugees from El Salvador, or nurses from the Philippines, the decision to leave behind all that is familiar is no easier than it was for Italian or Irish immigrants a century ago. And like their earlier counterparts, today's immigrants must struggle with the question of whether their stay in the United States or Canada will be permanent. It is safe to say that every immigrant has at some time wrestled with that question. The chapters that follow will consider how the members of some of America's most prominent immigrant groups decided that issue, impinged upon by the various circumstances that make their group's experience both singular and a larger part of a shared American heritage.

THE INCONVENIENCIES
THAT HAVE HAPPENED TO SOME PER-
SONS WHICH HAVE TRANSPORTED THEMSELVES

from *England* to *Virginia*, vvithout prouisions necessary to sustaine themselues, hath
greatly hindred the *Progresse* of that noble *Plantation*: For preuention of the like disorders
heereafter, that no man suffer, either through ignorance or misinformation; it is thought re-
quisite to publish this short declaration: wherein is contained a particular of such neces-
saries, as either priuate families or single persons shall haue cause to furnish themselues with, for their better
support at their first landing in Virginia; whereby also greater numbers may receiue in part,
directions how to prouide themselues.

Apparrell.

	li.	s.	d.
One Monmouth Cap	∞	01	10
Three falling bands	—	01	03
Three shirts	—	07	06
One waste-coate	—	02	02
One suite of Canuase	—	07	06
One suite of Frize	—	10	00
One suite of Cloth	—	15	00
Three paire of Irish stockins	—	04	00
Foure paire of shooes	—	08	c8
One paire of garters	—	00	10
One doozen of points	—	00	03
One paire of Canuase sheets	—	08	00
Seuen ells of Canuase, to make a bed and boulster, to be filled in *Virginia* 8.s.	—	08	00
One Rug for a bed 8.s. which with the bed seruing for two men, halfe is			
Fiue ells coorse Canuase, to make a bed at Sea for two men, to be filled with straw, iiij.s.	—	05	00
One coorse Rug at Sea for two men, will cost vj.s. is for one			
	04	00	00

Apparrell for one man, and so after the rate for more.

Victuall.

	li.	s.	d.
Eight bushels of Meale	02	00	00
Two bushels of pease at 3.s.	—	06	00
Two bushels of Oatemeale 4.s. 6.d.	—	09	00
One gallon of *Aquauitæ*	—	02	06
One gallon of Oyle	—	03	06
Two gallons of Vineger 1.s.	—	02	00
	03	03	00

For a whole yeere for one man, and so for more after the rate.

Armes.

	li.	s.	d.
One Armour compleat, light	—	17	00
One long Peece, fiue foot or fiue and a halfe, neere Musket bore	01	02	00
One sword	—	05	00
One belt	—	01	00
One bandaleere	—	01	06
Twenty pound of powder	—	18	00
Sixty pound of shot or lead, Pistoll and Goose shot	—	05	00
	03	09	06

For one man, but if halfe of your men haue armour is it sufficient so that all haue Peeces and swords.

Tooles.

	li.	s.	d.
Fiue broad howes at 2.s. a piece	—	10	—
Fiue narrow howes at 16.d. a piece	—	06	c8
Two broad Axes at 3.s. 8.d. a piece	—	07	c4
Fiue felling Axes at 18.d. a piece	—	07	06
Two steele hand sawes at 16.d. a piece	—	02	08
Two two-hand-sawes at 5.s. a piece	—	10	—
One whip-saw, set and filed with box, file, and wrest	—	10	—
Two hammers 12.d. a piece	—	02	00
Three shouels 18.d. a piece	—	04	06
Two spades at 18.d. a piece	—	03	—
Two augers 6.d. a piece	—	01	00
Sixe chissels 6.d. a piece	—	03	00
Two percers stocked 4.d. a piece	—	00	c8
Three gimlets 2.d. a piece	—	00	06
Two hatchets 21.d. a piece	—	03	06
Two froues to cleaue pale 18.d.	—	03	00
Two hand-bills 20. a piece	—	03	04
One grindlestone 4.s.	—	04	00
Nailes of all sorts to the value of	02	00	00
Two Pickaxes	—	03	—
	06	02	c8

For a family of 6. persons and so after the rate for more.

Houshold Implements.

	li.	s.	d.
One Iron Pot	c0	07	—
One kettle	—	06	—
One large frying-pan	—	02	c6
One gridiron	—	01	06
Two skillets	—	05	—
One spit	—	02	—
Platters, dishes, spoones of wood	—	04	—
	01	08	00

For a family of. 6. persons, and so for more or lesse after the rate.

For Suger, Spice, and fruit, and at Sea for 6.men. — | — | 12 | 06

So the full charge of Apparrell, Victuall, Armes, Tooles,
and houshold stuffe, and after this rate for each person,
will amount vnto about the summe of — | 12 | 10 | —
The passage of each man is — | 06 | 00 | —
The fraight of these prouisions for a man, will bee about
halfe a Tun, which is — | 01 | 10 | —

So the whole charge will amount to about — | 20 | 00 | 00

Nets, hookes, lines, and a tent must be added, if the number of people be greater, as also some kine.
And this is the vsuall proportion that the Virginia *Company doe
bestow vpon their Tenants which they send.*

Whosoeuer transports himselfe or any other at his owne charge vnto *Virginia*, shall for each person so transported before Midsummer 1625.
haue to him and his heires for euer fifty Acres of Land vpon a first, and fifty Acres vpon a second diuision.

Imprinted at London by FELIX KYNGSTON. 1622.

TO THE NEW WORLD AND BACK

Although the English and their descendants would eventually dominate North America, they made a slow start at settlement. For almost a century after Columbus's landfall at San Salvador in 1492, the English showed little interest in colonizing the New World. Preoccupied with establishing their power in Europe, England's monarchs were reluctant to pay the costs of sending settlers across the sea. Some people warned that there was little to be gained by going and that anyone who went would regret the day he first heard the word *America.*

By the late 1500s, several factors had combined to change people's minds. An ascendant merchant class stood ready to challenge the old nobility for political power and to furnish the leadership and the capital for settlements. The joint stock company, a financial organization akin to today's corporation, was perfected as a way to finance costly ventures. England's population grew faster than its economy, leaving many people without work.

The Protestant Reformation—the gospel of salvation through faith, rather than works, and a personal relationship with God, preached by Martin Luther, John Calvin, and others—also spurred American colonization in several ways. In its opposition to a monolithic ecclesiastical authority such as existed in the Catholic church, Protestantism encouraged the formation of dissident sects. When King Henry VIII broke with the pope and formed the Church of England in 1534, England became a Protestant nation by law. Even so, the Puritans, Protestant dissidents who wished to purify the church of ostentation and corruption, found themselves at odds with the Crown and with religious and civil authorities and were soon the target of repressive legislation. By the close of the 16th century, Puritans as well as Catholics were leaving England in the hope of finding a more tolerant atmosphere elsewhere.

Roanoke and Jamestown

In 1585 the 100 men of an English expedition outfitted and financed by the courtier and poet Sir Walter Raleigh landed on Roanoke Island, off the coast of what became North Carolina. Expecting to make a quick fortune by finding gold and trading with the Indians, the prospective colonists returned to England the very next year when it became apparent that they would have to plow fields and grow food in order to survive.

A year later, in 1587, a new group of English immigrants arrived in Roanoke. This time women and children accompanied the men, a strong indication that the colonists were intent on making their home in the New World. But supplies dispatched from England in 1588 never arrived, and when more Englishmen did reach Roanoke in 1590, they found its denizens vanished and the colony deserted. The fate of the Roanoke Island settlement remains a mystery.

Some years later the English tried again. In 1607 three ships carrying about a hundred men landed at a peninsula in the James River. The village they founded there was called Jamestown, after England's reigning monarch. The absence of women and children makes it likely that the immigrants intended their stay to be brief, probably only long enough to extract gold, copper, silver, and other precious metals from the virgin wilderness, as the charter granted by the Crown permitted them to do.

The settlers endured a trying first few months. The river's swamps bred malaria and mosquitoes; the colonists had landed too late in the year to grow sufficient food for the winter, and they quarreled among themselves over the division of labor and other responsibilities. By January, when reinforcements and supplies arrived from England, two-thirds of the settlers had died, and many of the survivors were considering heading home.

Life at Jamestown improved once the settlers learned how to cultivate tobacco, a product that soon found an eager market in England. Profits from the export and sale of "the weed" enabled Jamestown to prosper, and

The American painter Thomas Cole's The Notch of the White Mountains. *The first English settlers in the New World found a land replete with great natural beauty, but they often suffered from a sense of isolation unknown to them in the villages and cities of England.*

more settlers, including women, crossed the Atlantic to settle in Jamestown or to establish new settlements in the colony of Virginia. The introduction of slave labor from Africa also eased the life of the colonists, although most could not afford to keep slaves.

That they stayed does not prove that all the colonists were entirely content in their new home. Virginia Company records show that even after many years had passed some of the early settlers continued to think of themselves as temporary exiles and dreamed of going back to England. Although rich in land, game, timber, water, vegetation, and mineral resources, the New World seldom yielded its treasures to those unwilling to work, and many of the colonists were still more attracted by the idea of making a quick fortune than by the toil necessary to forge a new life. Robert Beverley, one of the first Virginians, wrote of his fellow settlers that they were more "concerned to fetch away the treasure than to form any colony."

Massachusetts Bay

Virginia was not the only place where the English settled in the New World. In 1607 a small settlement on the Kennebec River in Massachusetts lasted only a few months before its residents gave up and returned home. Thirteen years later, the *Mayflower*, carrying a group of Puritan dissenters known to future generations as the Pilgrims, made land at Plymouth Rock. Beginning in 1630 they were joined by thousands of their coreligionists and established the Massachusetts Bay Colony, which they hoped to make "as a city upon a hill," a moral beacon to the rest of the sinful world. The new colony's most important settlement was at Boston.

The northern colony differed in many ways from the Virginia settlement. Fleeing religious repression and fully intending to build a new life for themselves in the New World, the Puritans came as families. Whereas the first Virginians were predominantly males seeking riches or adventure, from the outset children, women, and older people were an integral part of life in the Massachusetts Bay Colony. Because many of the Virginians had lacked the money to pay for their voyage, they had agreed to work a number of years, usually from five to seven, in order to pay off the debt incurred for the trip, an arrangement known as indentured servitude. Few Massachusetts Bay immigrants arrived as indentured servants. Individuals from a cross section of occupations, including lawyers and clergymen, helped settle the first colony in New England.

As in Virginia, simple survival was initially the colonists' most important challenge. Land had to be cleared, fields plowed, crops sown and harvested. Wild game was abundant, but many Puritans feared to venture into New England's deep forests, believing them to be inhabited by Satan and his familiars as well as by unfriendly Indians. Plants and herbs used for medicine in England were not to be found in America. Indeed, the Pilgrims at first proved so inept at fending for themselves that they would not have survived their first winters had it not been for the assistance of the Indians. Despite the Indians' help, separation from friends and relatives and the familiarity of life in England made those first winters seem exceedingly long and bleak.

There is no doubt that hardship turned the thoughts of many toward England, and events of the 1640s made the homeland appear all the more desirable. When the long-simmering dispute between Parliament and the Crown over which would be the supreme political authority of England exploded into civil war in 1642, Puritans were among the Parliamentarians' staunchest supporters. The conflict is even sometimes referred to as the Puritan Revolution. The military victory and accession to power of the Parliamentarian general Oliver Cromwell, himself a Puritan, convinced many of the Massachusetts faithful that the time was right for their return. An economic depression that plagued Mas-

A 1767 advertisement from Charleston, South Carolina, seeks the return of William Burns, a runaway indentured servant. Indentured servitude was a common way for impoverished Englishmen to pay for their passage to the New World.

Half of the Pilgrim settlers at Plymouth, Massachusetts, died during the colony's first bleak winter there.

sachusetts during the 1640s further stimulated the exodus. Although no records were kept of the number of colonists who departed, Thomas Hutchinson, who governed Massachusetts from 1771 to 1774, estimated that more people left the colony during the 1600s than entered. If the behavior of the first graduates of the colony's only university, Harvard, which was founded in 1636, was any indication, Hutchinson's surmise was probably correct. Although historian Samuel Eliot Morison said that Harvard was a "college of exiles," seven of the nine members of its first graduating class returned to England.

Others left the Massachusetts Bay Colony for the same reason that they had originally gone there—because of religious disagreements. While covetous of religious tolerance for themselves, the Puritans were reluctant to extend it to others. Newcomers were scrutinized to weed out those "unmeet to inhabit here." Members of the English separatist Protestant denomination known as the Quakers—who did not observe the sacraments, denied the authority of ordained clergy, refused to swear oaths, and would not bear arms—were often hounded and persecuted until they left the colony. Some who clashed with the Massachusetts Bay hierarchy simply moved on to found new settlements, as did Anne

Hutchinson, who left Massachusetts Bay after a doctrinal dispute with church leaders there. Henry Vane, a former governor of the colony, returned to England after he fell out with his successor. Francis Higginson, who came from England to serve as a minister in Massachusetts Bay, demanded that his contract include a provision that his family be provided free passage home at any time during his first two years. One man who arrived in the colony in 1630 quipped that he heard less talk about how to get to heaven than about how to get back to England.

A New Nation

Talk about departure did not stop other immigrants from continuing to come to America. The population grew steadily through the 1600s, reaching 250,000 (including African slaves) by 1700. Growth was even faster in the 18th century. By 1770 the population of the 13 American colonies had topped 2.2 million, a figure that would have been even larger if all the immigrants had remained. Once the inhabitants of the 13 colonies took up arms in 1775 in order to achieve their independence from Great Britain, those colonists who sided with the mother country were particularly likely to leave. Although the exact number of early Americans who favored continuing as a British colony is unknown, one estimate placed the total at up to 18 percent of the white population. Called Loyalists or Tories, the pro-British colonists were not popular with their neighbors who favored independence. Tories frequently found themselves the target of mob violence directed against their person or property, particularly in Boston and New York City. Some states enacted anti-Tory legislation that allowed land, buildings, and businesses owned by Loyalists to be seized and sold.

When the Treaty of Paris ended the war in 1783, some Loyalists expected their land and property to be returned, but they were disappointed. The treaty specified that the new American Congress would "recommend" that the states restore the property seized, but it was little more than a token gesture. Victorious Americans were in no mood to give anything back to the defeated enemy, and few Tories were able to successfully reclaim anything. In all, about 100,000 Loyalists left America for Britain or Canada during the war and its aftermath. In a population of less than 3 million, that meant that 1 out of every 25 individuals departed.

Immigrants, Not Colonists

British immigration to North America did not end with the transformation of the British colonies into the independent United States of America, but the type of Britisher who came changed. During the first decades of the 1700s, the majority of British immigrants came from London and northern England, areas that were experiencing economic growth. Many of those who came possessed skills, such as carpentry and shoemaking, that they hoped to use in America. The overt hostility that characterized relations between the United States and Great Britain from 1775 to 1815 greatly slowed British immigration, but it picked up again once the two nations began to settle their differences following the War of 1812. British immigration to the United States then increased steadily, with some slight fluctuations, through the rest of the century. The typical new immigrant was likely to be a farmer or craftsman from rural southern or western England; most came with their families. Immigration records show that in 1831 only about one out of every four British newcomers braved America alone; those who did were usually young males trained as engineers or cotton spinners. Most of these immigrants intended to make their home permanently in the United States, as the presence of their families indicates.

But by the late 19th century, bachelors constituted a much larger percentage of English immigrants, and they were less likely than their predecessors to have a skill.

The 1855 woodcut at top contrasts America's need for manpower—the sign at the U.S. immigration station at Castle Garden says that 1 million men are wanted—with England's surplus population. Many members of the English working class emigrated in order to avoid the poverty portrayed in the 1859 drawing of a London street scene at bottom.

Often day laborers, miners, or construction workers, they came to America intending to work for a while and then return home.

Once the great wave of immigration to the United States began in the 1840s, English immigrants tended to be overlooked, for several reasons. Although many English continued to make the journey across the Atlantic, the great majority of them in the filthy, pestilent steerage compartments of overbooked steamships, they were outdone in terms of numbers by other groups, particularly the Germans, the Irish, and later the Italians. Because they were generally fair skinned, spoke English, and practiced Protestantism, British immigrants generally had an easier time assimilating in a nation intensely suspicious of foreign tongues; swarthy, yellow, or black skin; and Catholicism or other non-Protestant religions. The number of English immigrants peaked in the 1880s, when almost 80,000 came to these shores each year, but they seldom felt the full brunt of the prejudice and discrimination that greeted other immigrants at that time. Their ability to achieve professional and economic success in their new home is indicated by the fact that a higher percentage of the English were able to become doctors, lawyers, or engineers than any other immigrant group. So successful were the English at blending into American society that they are sometimes referred to as the "invisible immigrants."

Why They Left

Although the English may have had an easier time assimilating than other immigrant groups, they were not immune to homesickness. As had been the case with the earliest British settlers in the New World, many found that their expectations far exceeded reality, an insight expressed by a British immigrant in Iowa as awakening "to a painful realization that our imagination had run away with our judgment." Not all British were able to enter the professions; the great majority worked as farmers, miners, or in construction. Life on the prairies and in the West, where many English went in search of land, proved particularly hard to bear. A Britisher who had settled in Illinois in 1817 fled back to England, disillusioned by the "dirt, bad cooking and discomfort of every kind."

Such dissatisfaction was not merely regional. The Englishman Charles Hooton's published account of his attempt to resettle in Texas in the 1840s was a virtual litany of the horrors and shortcomings of the Lone Star

Many English immigrants returned home because they arrived in the New World thoroughly unprepared for the realities of life there. Entitled "The Emigrant's Welcome to Canada," the cartoon above lampoons the naïveté of the greenhorn settler, whose pack contains dancing shoes and silk stockings rather than the snowshoes and winter gear that would be more appropriate.

State.   His avowed purpose in writing, Hooton explained, was to "lay my experiences of Texas before the world, and to the utmost of my ability persuade, through the influence of facts, any projecting Emigrants from following in the same fatal footsteps."   The would-be Texan had few fond memories of his American adventure: "May I never again see such ruin of body and fortune, such wreck of heart, as it was my fate to witness in Texas!"

Some found the Northeast no more hospitable. John Pearson left England in 1821 with his wife and 18 pet dogs. His party arrived in Philadelphia in the midst of a wilting heat wave that promptly killed 16 of the dogs. Saddened but undeterred for the moment, the Pearsons set out for Pittsburgh. Along the way they came across several messages left by compatriots who had preceded them.   One such communication, scrawled across a bridge, seemed an ominous harbinger to the eager new-comers. "England with all thy faults, I love thee still," it read, and by November the Pearsons were echoing its sentiments. That month they returned to England, leaving their two surviving dogs behind.

Developments in transportation made it even easier for the English to return home. In the second half of the 19th century, steamships made the trip from England to the United States (and vice versa) in about 10 days. The phenomenon of the English repeater—those immigrants who made several trips to the United States to work, returning to England when their pockets or bellies were full—was well established by 1880. By that time the rate of English immigration depended less on events in England than on fluctuations in the American economy. In times of prosperity in the United States, immigrants flocked here, confident that they would be able to find work and make money. During downturns, such as that which plagued the American economy during the early

Immigrants were particularly hard hit by downturns in the American economy. This wood engraving after a drawing by the American artist Winslow Homer shows the homeless huddled together in a New York City police station during the depression of 1873. Hard times convinced many English to return home.

Texas seems to have been particularly hard for the English to bear, as evidenced by Charles Hooton's written accounts and this 19th-century cartoon satirizing the frustration felt by two English settlers unable to obtain one of the familiar comforts of home.

1890s, immigration slowed and the number of returnees increased.

In the 20th century, transatlantic travel became even easier, and English immigration remained steady. An average of more than 200,000 English per decade entered the United States during the first 9 decades of the 20th century. The ease of travel also made it relatively simple for immigrants to return home, which many British continued to do, whether for reasons of homesickness, dashed expectations, economic changes, or fulfillment of their ambitions here.

Irish peasants in the 1880s. Under English rule, Ireland's Catholics, although constituting the great majority of the population, were an oppressed people. In the countryside, most lived in rude cottages rented from Protestant landlords.

IRISH AND SWEDES

During the 1800s immigration from Ireland constituted the first of the great European mass migrations that would transform the character of U.S. society, but by that time the Irish had been coming to North America almost as long as the British. Their reasons for doing so were severalfold. By the 17th century and the time of the first permanent settlements in the New World, England had maintained a military and political presence in Ireland for more than 400 years. Legislation passed in the 1500s prohibited the Irish from speaking Gaelic, their native tongue; outlawed the Catholic mass (the overwhelming majority of Irish were Roman Catholic), and declared all the nation's land to be the rightful property of the English king. That same century also witnessed the first efforts at plantation, as the British policy of driving the Irish from their land and repopulating it with Protestant settlers from Scotland and England was known. Oliver Cromwell, whose military campaigns in Ireland during the 1640s were notorious for their brutality, sought to drive all the Irish north and west of the River Shannon, to the barren and rocky province of Connaught. Irish found east or south of the Shannon after May 1, 1654, could legally be killed or transported into slavery in the British colonies in the West Indies. The Penal Laws enacted by the British between 1695 and 1727 prevented Irish Catholics from bearing weapons, owning or inheriting land, receiving an education, entering a profession, or voting in elections. The Catholic clergy was formally banned, although the English never succeeded in eradicating Catholicism. By 1775 the Penal Laws and the plantation policy had worked so well that Irish Catholics owned only five percent of the land in their own nation.

Thousands Are Sailing

Under such conditions, it is not surprising that many Irish Catholics were willing to try their luck elsewhere. No precise figures are available, but Irish Catholics had already begun immigrating to North America by the early 1600s. During the colonial years, the Irish constituted the largest non-English immigrant group, but in the New World, the Irish again found themselves subjugated and repressed by a Protestant governing class. The English in the colonies were little more tolerant of Irish Catholics than they had been in Ireland, and several colonies passed legislation prohibiting Irish Catholic immigration. Still, the Irish continued to come, and their dislike for the English served the colonies well during the revolutionary war, when they fought so fiercely for American independence that the British commander in chief, Sir Henry Clinton, lamented that he was unable to recruit troops from "whence the rebels themselves drew most of their best soldiers—I mean the Irish." The Irish contribution to American independence was so great that a pro-British member of the Irish Parliament lamented in 1784 that "America was lost by Irish emigrants."

The great wave of Irish immigration began in the 1820s. In that decade more than 50,000 Irish, driven across the ocean by a depression in agricultural prices and a rise in population that exacerbated the continued economic hardship in their own land, came to the United States. Over the next 10 years that number quadrupled, and the Irish represented nearly 35 percent of all the immigrants admitted to the United States during the 1830s. But Irish immigration did not peak until the late 1840s and early 1850s, following the great potato famine, which through starvation and forced emigration reduced Ireland's population by almost one-quarter.

The Great Hunger

By the mid-1800s, the great majority of Irish Catholics were still impoverished tenant farmers and agricultural laborers. For most, the potato, which took little labor to cultivate and produced a high yield per acre, was their primary staple. Potatoes and milk formed the bulk of the average Irishman's diet, and by 1845 potatoes were the sole food of one-third of the population. When potato blight destroyed virtually the entire crop that year, and part of the crop failed again the next two years, large segments of the population, particularly in the rural west, were sentenced to starvation. Such diseases as dysentery, yellow fever, scurvy, typhus, and cholera claimed almost as many victims as hunger. Hundreds of thousands of others crowded Irish ports seeking passage to America, but those who found a ship received no guarantee that they had eluded death. Disease ran rampant on shipboard, and by the time the notorious "coffin ships" reached New York or Boston as many as 20 percent of the passengers might have perished. The coffin ships notwithstanding, nearly 1.5 million Irish immigrated to the United States between 1841 and 1851, establishing a pattern of Irish immigration that has persisted until this day. Ireland's population dropped from 8.1 million in 1841 to fewer than 3.5

In the United States, Irish immigrants were caricatured as lantern-jawed, simianlike creatures, notable for their brawn and capacity for alcoholic drink. "Paddy's Ladder to Wealth in a Free Country" reads the caption to the cartoon above; it indicates that the Irish immigrant's willingness as a manual laborer was seen as his only means of success.

million in 1980, a decrease attributable primarily to emigration.

About equal numbers of men and women immigrated from Ireland, although the large number of single women among them made the Irish unique in that regard. Those Irish who came to the United States before the Great Hunger were more likely to possess skills than their countrymen who came later, most of whom were agricultural laborers. Most were literate. Even in 1850, when the typical Irish immigrant was most likely to be an unskilled peasant, an impressive 75 percent of all Irish immigrants could read and write. The difficulties of an agricultural existence in the homeland had given most Irish their fill of rural living, so in the United States most settled in urban areas, primarily on the East Coast, where they worked in a variety of occupations. Prejudice and poverty made their lot a difficult one, and the Irish were stereotyped by the Protestant majority as drunken and violent, their religion ridiculed as popish superstition.

Despite their difficulty in achieving economic success in the United States—studies showed that in the late 19th century the Irish in Boston, then the city with the highest concentration of Irish Americans, were outperformed economically by every major immigrant group, as well as by the native born—a relatively small percentage of Irish returned to the homeland, no doubt because opportunity was even more restricted there. Only about 1 in 10 of those who came over between 1850 and 1900 returned home, but because the total number of immigrants was so high, the number of returnees amounted to hundreds of thousands.

Most of the Irish returnees fell into one of three categories. The first had intended to emigrate only temporarily in order to put aside some savings or to pay off old debts. After a few years of work in the New World, they took what they had earned and returned home. A second category returned because of unexpected developments at home. A son might go back to the homeland to take advantage of an inheritance or in

 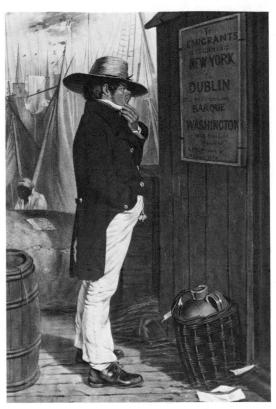

response to a call from a sick family member or friend. This group included almost half the male returnees. The members of the third category returned because they were dissatisfied with life in America. Sometimes their complaints were general—the cities were too large or too dirty—but often it was a specific misfortune, such as the death of a spouse or a serious illness, that brought them home.

Those Irish immigrants who returned in the 1850s and 1860s tended to be skilled rather than unskilled workers, perhaps because they found it easier to save enough for the trip back. Most were still in their twenties and thirties, young enough to begin anew at home. Only about one in four returned in family groups, sometimes bringing with them children born in America. Among the sadder cases on the passenger lists were widows with

Before and after: (Left) Clad in rags, an Irishman on the Dublin docks examines a poster extolling the benefits of immigration to the United States. (Right) Having achieved some measure of success in the New World, as indicated by his spotless new clothes, the same Irishman pauses on a quay in New York City to contemplate a triumphant return to the old country.

In this 1843 cartoon, Daniel O'Connell, a politician revered as the Liberator of Catholic Ireland, calls upon his compatriots who have emigrated to return home. The Irish community in America lent much support to the effort to free the homeland from English rule, and many Irish returned home to join in the fight.

children. The death of a husband made many women reconsider their prospects in America, and going back to relatives who could help often seemed preferable to raising a family alone.

Overall, the returnees made little discernible impact on Ireland. In other countries, returnees introduced new farming methods or taught new skills they had acquired abroad, but not in Ireland. Few of the immigrants returned wealthy. Those returnees who went back to farming worked plots no larger than the average. In spite of the fact that they had uprooted themselves and endured two trips across the Atlantic, the Irish returnees did not appear significantly better off than those who had never left. However, considering how many Irish perished during the Great Hunger, the returnees had profited in one fashion—they were alive.

Swedish Immigrants

Although Swedes settled in Delaware in the 1630s, they did not become a significant part of American life for

200 years. Only in the 1840s, when hard times hit Sweden, did emigration grow. Some farmers sold their land and took their money and their families off to start anew in America. Those who had land to sell were fortunate. Overpopulation and related economic forces had left much of the rural populace landless, and many of these peasants also emigrated. Others fled in search of religious freedom, as the Lutheran church was the only officially approved religion.

Most of the mid-19th-century Swedish immigrants left in family groups, a sure sign that they intended their exile to be permanent. Most of the young, single, male emigrants who left Sweden before 1860 were persons of some means—landowners, skilled craftsmen, and others who had access to funds and to information about prospects in America.

In *Reminiscences: The Story of an Emigrant*, Hans Mattson tells of leaving his farm in Sweden in 1851 at the age of 18. "At that time," he wrote, "America was little known in our part of the country, only a few persons having emigrated from the whole district. But we knew that it was a new country inhabited by a free and independent people, that it had a liberal government and great natural resources, and these inducements were sufficient for us."

After 17 years in America, most of them in Minnesota, Mattson returned to Sweden because, as he explained in his autobiography, "For many years I had desired to revisit the home of my childhood." He found enormous changes and was struck by the difference that railroads, which had been unknown in rural Sweden when he left, had made. At 35 years of age, Mattson had lived about half his life in the United States and half in Sweden, so he was equipped to make some comparisons. He quickly gave the advantage to his adopted land. "We Americans," he wrote as proudly as any native-born patriot, "hold that all power of government emanates from the people and that the officers of the government, from the president down to the village constable, are merely servants of the people." In Europe, he observed, people behaved as though any privilege they received from their rulers was bestowed as some great favor, but in the United States he had witnessed humble citizens who went before their government officials "with head erect" and demanded that "such and such things be done according to the law." Mattson marveled at how lowly Swedish bureaucrats flaunted their power, and he commented wryly that the governor of one small Swedish province "the size of half a dozen of our counties appears with more pomp and style than any governors of our great [American] states."

It might be expected that such a negative impression of Sweden would have sent Mattson back to Minnesota permanently, but like many immigrants he had mixed emotions. Over the next few years, he returned to Sweden several times and even enrolled his children in schools there. In spite of his praises for his new country and his reference to himself as an American, the country of his birth exerted a special pull, one that he was unable to ignore. Nor did he want his children to grow up ignorant of it and its customs.

Still, whenever Mattson returned to Sweden, he encouraged other immigrants to go to the United States. By the 1860s, he found many willing to follow him. One-fourth of Sweden's total population emigrated in the late 19th century.

These emigrants differed in several ways from those who had left in the 1840s and 1850s. Fewer families and more young, single men and women left to look for work. By the 1880s unmarried individuals made up 70 percent of the total number of Swedish immigrants. Overpopulation continued to be the single largest cause of immigration. Farms, repeatedly subdivided among children, eventually became too small to feed a family. By 1870 nearly half of the rural population was landless, and young people were forced to look for jobs elsewhere.

A variety of causes continued to drive Swedes from their homeland even when prospects in the United States

Hans Mattson, whose memoirs, Reminiscences: The Story of an Emigrant, *poignantly delineate the divided loyalties often felt by the immigrant.*

were not promising. In the 1890s, when a depression left many Americans jobless and inspired members of other immigrant groups, such as the English, to return home, nearly 230,000 Swedes arrived to swell the ranks of those looking for work. In the decades that followed, networks of their compatriots continued to furnish prospective Swedish immigrants with information on a variety of important subjects, such as how to locate a job and find housing. This advice was welcomed by young Swedes unhappy at home with the prospect of military service, restrictions that barred them from voting, and low wages.

Traditionally, young, single immigrants in search of work are good candidates for repatriation. Unlike families, they often head for areas undergoing rapid economic growth because that is where work is likely to be found. Such areas are also sensitive to economic fluctuations, and when downturns occur, industries there respond quickly by laying off workers. Facing unemployment, these single people, unencumbered by spouses and children, can pack up and leave.

Something akin to this scenario took place in the 1890s, when more than 47,000 Swedes returned home—a number equal to 23 percent of those who had journeyed to America in that decade. Between 1900 and 1910, the number of repatriates decreased to 20 percent of the immigrants, but in the following decade it climbed to 46 percent. In other words, about half as many men

Sent home by Swedish immigrants who helped settle Redvers in the western Canadian province of Saskatchewan, this postcard plays on the popular notion that everything was bigger and better in America.

TAKING OUR GEESE TO MARKET

17

and women returned to Sweden as came to America. In the 1920s the rate of repatriation was 30 percent.

Many explanations have been offered for these figures. Perhaps the most important is that travel between the two countries became easier to arrange after the Swedish-American steamship line was established in 1915. Only in the 1930s, when the Great Depression cut immigration to a trickle, did Swedes abandon the two-way migration that Hans Mattson had described so well.

The Reverend Peter Widvey and his family, Swedish immigrants, on their homestead in Custer County, Nebraska. Many immigrants returned home after being deterred by the enormity of the effort required to turn America's prairie and woodlands into usable farmland.

Chinese immigrants began arriving on the West Coast at a time when laborers were needed to build railroads and to mine gold and other precious minerals. This photograph was taken in 1852 at the Auburn Ravine mine in California.

UNWELCOME GUESTS: THE ASIANS

If immigrants from Asia brought with them a different set of expectations than did the Europeans, they also received a much harsher reception than did their European counterparts. Easily identifiable as outsiders, virtually every sizable Asian immigrant group—Chinese, Japanese, Filipinos, and Koreans—found themselves the targets of discriminatory legislation that sought to deny them entrance, prevented them from obtaining citizenship, forbade them to marry non-Asian women, and prohibited them from working at certain jobs. Because so many of the Asians stayed only a brief time in North America—both by design and because of the treatment they received—they soon became known as sojourners or middlemen.

Chinese Sojourners

Although a handful of Chinese adventurers came to North America aboard ships of various nations as early as the 1500s, the Chinese did not make a major impact here until the 1850s. The discovery of gold at Sutter's Mill in northern California in 1848 drew fortune-seeking men and women from all over the world, including many men from South China, especially the region around Canton. These Chinese would-be prospectors renamed San Francisco "Gold Mountain," a name that was eventually applied to all of California and even the entire continent.

The push to leave China was at least as strong as the pull of Gold Mountain. The heavy taxes imposed by the oppressive, corrupt Qing dynasty weighed heavily on the peasants, as did a series of floods and epidemics that resulted in widespread misery in the countryside. England's defeat of China in the Opium War (1839–42) and the increased influence of the Western nations helped open up the country not only to trade with other countries but also to information about the rest of the world. The Taiping Rebellion, which lasted from 1851 to 1864 and led to the death of 20 million people and the dislocation of countless millions more, helped break down old economic arrangements and destroy traditional ways.

It is no wonder that North America's West Coast was a magnet for the Chinese and other immigrant groups in the 1850s. The region developed rapidly as thousands poured in almost overnight. Many came seeking a fortune in gold, while others recognized that there was money to be made in providing services for those who flocked west. Who would cook the food and iron the shirts for those who were seeking gold? The answer, in many cases, was immigrant labor. One story had it that laundry service was so difficult to find in California that some men shipped their shirts to Hawaii for a wash and starch.

United States immigration officials recorded the arrival of about 300,000 Chinese between 1850 and 1882, when new legislation halted much Chinese immigration. Few of these were merchants or skilled workers—most came as common laborers without their wives or families. Chinese immigration of that period is remarkable for its high preponderance of males. In 1860, there were 18 Chinese men for every Chinese woman in the United States, and by 1890 the figure was even higher—nearly 27 to 1.

Chinese men who spent most of their adult life separated from their family found that they had made a great sacrifice. Betty Lee Sung, who has studied Chinese Americans, concluded that the men led sad lives, "denied the joys and cares of seeing their children grow up" and "condemned to a life . . . shorn of love and warmth."

Chinese men built America's railroads, tended truck farms, and pioneered new fishing methods along the Pacific coast, but for many reasons, they received little recognition for their contributions. Some had gone into debt for their passage over and had little recourse when contractors bargained their work away at unfair rates. Marked as different from the Caucasian majority by their skin color and facial characteristics, the Chinese were the victims of legislation barring them not only from the professions—few had the necessary education or training anyway—but also from more lucrative unskilled positions in mines or factories. Exploited by Chinese entrepreneurs and by American racists, Chinese workers earned little, worked under unhealthy and often dangerous conditions, and lived in substandard housing.

Prejudice in America reinforced the Chinese determination to return home. Most Chinese men had never intended to abandon their homeland or old traditions

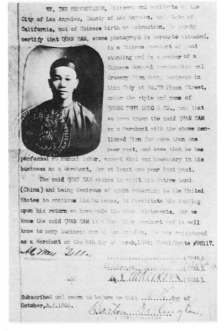

Once the Chinese Exclusion Act went into effect in 1882, Chinese who wished to visit family and friends in the homeland needed documentation to ensure that they would be allowed to reenter the United States.

VOL. VII.—No. 175. JULY 14, 1880. Price.10 Cents.

"What fools these Mortals be!"
MIDSUMMER-NIGHTS-DREAM

Puck

PUBLISHED BY
KEPPLER & SCHWARZMANN

NEW YORK
OFFICE No.21—23 WARREN S

WHERE BOTH PLATFORMS AGREE.—NO VOTE—NO USE TO EITHER PARTY.

According to this 1880 cartoon, proposed legislation that would end or severely restrict further Chinese immigration was likely to become law because as the Chinese were not citizens and thus could not vote, they were of no political use to either the Democrats or the Republicans.

but only to work long enough to save money to take back with them. In line with the beliefs of Confucianism, the system of ethical beliefs that regulated Chinese society, wives stayed behind to look after children, care for the husband's parents, and tend ancestral shrines. Sojourners showed little incentive to learn English or participate in American politics. The organizations most of them trusted were those that came from home and were based on either clan membership or region of origin.

The determination of the Chinese to remain outside mainstream American society increased their chances of becoming subjects of ridicule and unfair treatment. Jests about the men's braided hair and charges that they ate all sorts of strange foods, including rats, were among the milder insults. Legislation was passed so as to make their lives more difficult and their labor less profitable. For example, Chinese had traditionally carried heavy loads on poles across their shoulders, but in 1870 the city of San Francisco passed a law banning this method of transport. Sometimes the discrimination turned violent, as in 1871 when a riot in Los Angeles resulted in the death of 19 Chinese men.

In the 1870s, the outcry against Chinese workers grew louder and uglier. American laborers complained that the "coolies," as unskilled Chinese laborers were pejoratively known, worked for lower wages than Americans were willing to accept, and racists charged that the Chinese would never assimilate. So long as California needed labor, demands for barring the Chinese had little chance of succeeding, but by 1880 more American settlers had come west and the need for Chinese laborers decreased. In 1882, Congress passed the Chinese Exclusion Act, the first such federal law aimed at one national group. The act suspended the further admission of Chinese laborers for 10 years and also prohibited foreign-born Chinese from becoming citizens. Chinese merchants, students, and professionals were still al-

(continued on page 57)

Overleaf:
A restaurant sign in Tel Aviv symbolizes the "return" of thousands of Jewish Americans to their new homeland of Israel. After World War II, few American Jews returned to the countries from which they had immigrated. After 1948, however, with the creation of the modern state of Israel, that country offered the opportunity to share in the birth of a nation founded on the precepts of the Jewish faith. Today there are many reminders in Israel of this American heritage. At right: Members of the Jewish War Veterans of America and other American immigrants to Israel celebrate American Independence Day at a Fourth of July picnic in Jerusalem.

Israel abounds with reminders of American culture and commerce.
Above: American immigrants watch "Dynasty" on Israeli television.
At right: Families sample American ice cream in Jerusalem (above) and
Tel Aviv.

54

An American immigrant family in Jerusalem: Mother and son sample the books at the Jerusalem public library, where the English book collection is sponsored by the Association of Americans and Canadians in Israel. After reading in a Jerusalem park, the family encounters traces of Israel's Middle Eastern heritage, as camels and donkeys pass by in the street.

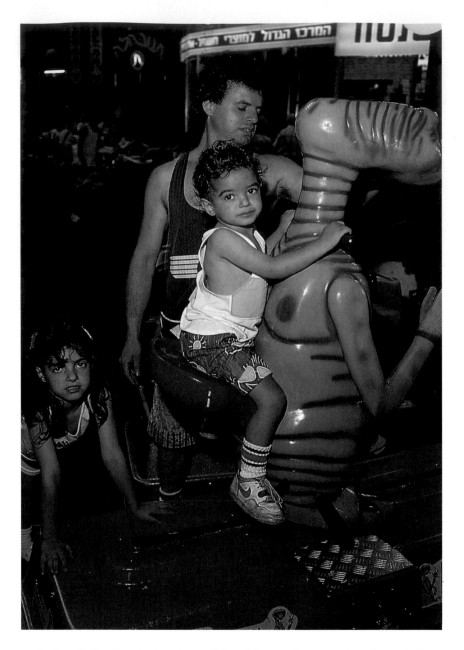

An Israeli family who immigrated from New York tour a shopping mall in Tel Aviv, where a ride based on the movie character E. T. offers a reminder of America.

(continued from page 48)

lowed to enter the United States legally. Of course, more than one enterprising worker attempted to pass himself off as a member of one of the accepted groups. One often-told story, of uncertain origin, described how one Chinese man was stopped by American officials and asked what he was doing in the United States. He replied, "Business."

"Well," the American official continued. "If you are here on business, how did you get those calluses on your hands?"

"From handling so much money," was the quick retort.

Once the Exclusion Act went into effect, many Chinese hesitated to risk a trip home because they feared being denied reentry. Later, when an earthquake destroyed city records in San Francisco, men would claim to have been born in the United States, which would make them citizens, and would then insist on the right to travel to China and return. When American courts upheld the right of admission for the foreign-born children of American-born Chinese, a clever scheme called the "paper son" arrangement was devised to make every trip home pay. Upon their return to the United States, Chinese men who had visited home would falsely report that they had fathered a son during their trip, thus creating an eligibility slot for the admission of that son at some future date. The documentation for that slot would then be sold to an ambitious young

Most Chinese immigrants retained strong ties to the homeland. Those who were unable to write employed the services of a public scribe to write home for them, as seen in this late-19th-century photograph taken in San Francisco's Chinatown.

countryman who wished to gain entrance to the United States.

Certain historians have concluded that almost all the Chinese immigrants who came to America in the 19th century meant to return home. If this is true, as the high percentage of male immigrants suggests, then the most interesting question is why so many of the Chinese stayed. By 1900, the U.S. Census counted nearly 90,000 persons "of the Chinese race," including immigrants and their children and grandchildren.

Because of their so-called sojourner mentality, most Chinese Americans maintained economic ties with their homeland and sent sizable amounts of money back. They also kept informed of political developments in China. Chinese in the United States and Canada helped finance the Sunning Railroad in the Sze Yap region, and those who were educated abroad but denied jobs returned home to pursue their careers.

Although some Chinese could still enter the United States legally after the Chinese Exclusion Act, most were barred until 1943. That year, while China was helping the United States win World War II, the barrier was finally lowered. A token number of 105 Chinese were allowed to enter the United States, and those already legally resident were permitted to become citizens. It was not until 1965 that the Chinese gained equal footing with non-Asian immigrants and were granted the same ceiling for entry to the United States. Many of those who immigrated after 1965 did so with their families, and the numbers of males and females in Chinese-American communities were equal by 1970, a sure sign that the sojourner mentality had changed and that the Chinese now meant to stay.

The Japanese

For centuries, Japan adhered to a policy of strict isolation, remaining closed to outside contact and forbidding its people to travel abroad. These practices, initiated in 1600, came to a forced end in 1853 with the

arrival of four U.S. gunships under the command of Matthew Perry. By the 1880s, Japan was emulating Western ways in an effort to build its economic and military strength and had begun to allow its subjects to go abroad to find work. Difficulties in Japan, especially overpopulation and unemployment in some of the farm districts, encouraged the government to enter into an arrangement with Hawaiian sugarcane growers. Japan agreed to supply the men needed on the Hawaiian plantations to grow and harvest sugarcane. They would be paid about nine dollars per month and receive food, lodging, medical care, and cooking fuel. A month's labor was calculated at 26 days, equal to a 6-day workweek plus 2 Sundays a month. To a Japanese worker without a job, $9 a month sounded like a lot of money, but it was considerably less than the $13.50 that the average farm worker earned in the United States. Still, by living frugally, mending and remending his clothes, the Japanese worker might hope to save a few hundred dollars, enough to begin building a house or to buy some land when he returned to Japan.

Thousands of Japanese men made the trip to Hawaii—29,000 in 1894 alone—but for most of them, plantation work was disappointing. Tending to acres and acres of sugarcane on brown, unshaded earth under the scorching Hawaiian sun made for exhausting work. Forced to sleep in sheds and to labor under the direction

Much of the labor on Hawaii's sugarcane plantations was performed by Japanese immigrants, many of whom intended to stay only long enough to make some money with which to return home.

When the United States became involved in World War II in December 1941, Japanese Americans living on the West Coast were forced to leave their homes and were interned in detention camps. These Japanese are having their luggage inspected upon arrival at the internment camp at Santa Anita, California.

of whip-bearing overseers, the Japanese had few effective ways of fighting to attain higher wages or more livable working conditions. Some deserted; others organized themselves so as to present a united front. According to author Lawrence Fuchs, one Japanese man was killed by his co-workers when he refused to honor an agreement not to outdo them in the fields.

Although enough Japanese remained in Hawaii to make them the single largest ethnic group there by 1896, their intention to someday return to their home islands helped motivate them to retain many of the traditions of the homeland. Even in their rickety sleeping quarters, they built shrines for remembering their deceased parents, as prescribed in the rites of Shinto, one of Japan's predominant religions.

The number of Japanese who made their way to the mainland United States was only a fraction of those who immigrated to Hawaii. Because they concentrated along the West Coast (Los Angeles County had the highest percentage—two percent of its total population in 1920) and in a few kinds of jobs (railroads, canneries, mining, fishing, meat packing, and especially truck farming), they often suffered from the same type of discrimination as did the Chinese. Both in Hawaii and on the mainland, the reluctance of the Japanese to commit themselves to building a permanent life in America left them as middlemen, frequent travelers between the Old World and the New World but fully a part of neither.

Those whom the immigrants left behind fully expected their kinsmen and countrymen to achieve great success in America, and more than one son remained in America rather than lose face by returning as a failure. In the novel *Samurai*, the Japanese-American writer Hisako Matsubara describes how one young bridegroom, Nagayuki, went to California in the early 1900s because his adopted father (who also happened to be his father-in-law) commanded him to do so. The bride's family had once been wealthy but had fallen into

bankruptcy. Having no son of their own, they looked to Nagayuki to bring back the gold that would help them retrieve family treasures.

In America, Nagayuki soon found that his Japanese law degree meant nothing, and he ended up slaving away in a cannery. Ashamed to return, he waited for 60 years. In the meantime, his father-in-law dissolved Nagayuki's marriage and had the daughter remarried to a wealthy man. When Nagayuki did finally go back, an old and broken man, he had nothing to show for his life but worn-out suitcases full of faded letters. The once proud and fiercely intelligent man now preferred to sit quietly and smile while his disappointed relatives wondered to themselves why he had not done better.

To limit the number of immigrants like Nagayuki, the United States entered into a pact with Japan in 1908, the so-called Gentlemen's Agreement. Without actually barring Japanese as a national group, the United States achieved the same result by persuading Japan to allow only a token number of workers to leave each year. Japanese immigration, which had been about 30,000 in 1907, immediately dropped by nearly half and then fell to about 3,000 in 1909. The number of Japanese returning to Japan also fell, although not as rapidly because there were still several thousand workers in the United States who had been planning to go back. By 1913, repatriation to Japan was negligible—fewer than 1,000 persons were returning each year.

Japanese internees line up for dinner at the detention camp at Manzanar, California, in May 1942. Despite the aspersions cast on their loyalty during World War II, most of the Japanese living in the United States chose to become citizens when that opportunity was finally made available to them in 1946.

Immigrant coal miners in Pennsylvania in 1900. Many of the so-called new immigrants who began coming to America around 1880 found work in the factories, mills, and mines of the northeastern United States.

THE NEW IMMIGRATION

Inspired in part by innovations in transportation, immigration took on a new character after 1880. New groups began coming to America at this time, possessed of different motives and different aims. The newly industrialized United States, with its coal mines, steel mills, railroads, and endless construction projects, had need of the manpower the newcomers provided. Canada was also building railroads and mining ores and precious metals, and its western provinces offered much unsettled land to attract settlers.

The primary innovation that spurred the new immigration was the development of the steamship as the chief mode of transatlantic travel. The steamship came into its heyday around 1860 or so and over the course of several decades replaced the stately clipper ships that had previously carried immigrants to their new lives. Its advantages included greater capacity (some could carry as many as 1,800 passengers), more predictable scheduling (steamships did not have to rely on favorable winds), and greater speed. Wind-powered vessels made the trip from Europe to North America in anywhere from one to three months. Steamships shortened the voyage to an average duration of 10 days. Because of these advantages, it was possible for steamships to profit by trafficking almost exclusively in an unusual cargo—humans. Whereas the great majority of the earlier immigrants traveled to North America in the holds of trade vessels that had unladed their cargo in Europe, the business of many steamship lines was the delivery of human passengers, not trade goods. Before the advent of the steamship, mass emigration was possible only from those nations that carried on extensive trade with the United States, namely the countries of northern and western Europe. Steamship travel made emigration from other parts of Europe possible.

For all these reasons, the introduction of the steamship had enormous consequences for Europe. It helped spread emigration fever to parts of the continent once considered immune to the contagion, and hundreds of thousands left each year. In 1885, not an atypical year, more than 350,000 Europeans landed in the United States—fully 10 times the number that arrived in an average year during the 1830s, when only sailing ships plied the seas. Slowly, steamship travel resulted in a change in the immigrants' countries of origin. In 1882, as had been the case for most of the 19th century, the great majority—87 percent—of the immigrants to the United States came from northern and western Europe, with Germany, Ireland, England, and Sweden sending the most. Twenty-five years later, the situation was greatly changed. Eighty-one percent of the immigrants to the United States in 1907 were from southern and eastern Europe. For the first time, Italians, Russians, and the many Slavic peoples who fell under the rule of the Austro-Hungarian Empire were in the forefront of immigration. Also for the first time, the United States became home to sizable Slavic, Jewish, and Mediterranean populations.

Just as steamship travel made immigration less difficult, so did it make the return home easier for those immigrants who grew homesick, were dissatisfied with their lives in the New World, or had accomplished what they set out to do. The relative ease of travel encouraged people to move back and forth between continents, and "bird of passage," the name given someone who immigrated and then returned, became a household phrase. Like jet aircraft in the 20th century, the steamship changed people's ideas about distances and travel.

Advances in transportation facilitated America's industrial development. The rise in immigration corresponded to America's need for manpower to do the dangerous, dirty, and low-paying work in its mines, factories, and mills. Strong backs were also needed to build the continent's railroads, subways, and highways. At the same time, thousands of Europeans, many of them young and strong, were looking to make a fresh start elsewhere. In Italy, political unification had failed to remedy the poverty and political repression that plagued the mostly illiterate peasantry in the southern part of the nation. Poles, Croatians, Serbs, Czechs, Hungarians, and other eastern Europeans also fled crushing poverty as well as the domination of their homeland by a foreign oppressor. Jews fled Russia by the thousands to escape a heightening of the brutal oppression that had long been their lot. By the last quarter of the 19th century, nearly one in four of America's nonfarm workers had been born abroad, a percentage that would increase over the next decades.

In North America, the shift in the flow of immigrants aroused considerable attention, much of it unfavorable. Termed new immigrants to distinguish them from the old immigrants who had preceded them, the southern and central Europeans were the subject of much criticism by other Americans, many of whose ancestors had themselves immigrated not long before. The new immigrants were reviled for their appearance—they tended to be shorter and darker of skin than the old immigrants; their religion—many were Catholic, whereas the United States was overwhelmingly Protestant; and their alleged clannishness and insularity—it was said that the new immigrants preferred to huddle together in urban ghettos rather than move out into American society.

Not surprisingly, those immigrants who intended to stay only temporarily tended to congregate in enclaves—Greektowns, Little Hungaries, or Little Italies—in the large cities, where they could count on receiving warmer treatment than the larger society would give. There they had little need for English—they could find a job, buy their groceries, and converse with co-workers and neighbors in the language their mothers had taught them. Obtaining citizenship and voting in American elections held little interest for the majority of them. In order to save as much money as possible, the birds of passage lived frugally, spending less than half of what they earned so that they could send the rest back home. Some Americans charged that these enclaves were unsavory places, that with so many single men living there the neighborhoods became rowdy havens for gambling, prostitution, and drunkenness. Others were angered by the immigrants' habit of sending money back to the home country. Money earned in America should remain in America, they argued.

For a variety of reasons, temporary immigrants became the subject of enormous debate in the United States during the last part of the 19th century. Eventually, they would play an important part in convincing Americans to severely restrict immigration. Two of the immigrant groups that drew the ire of nativist Americans were the Jews and the Greeks.

The Jews

Jewish immigrants constituted a significant part of the new immigration. Jews had many reasons to seek a new life in the New World. They were the target of virulent racial prejudice and extremely repressive legislation in most of the nations of Europe. In Russia, where 75 percent of the Jewish immigrants came from, they were confined by government edict to residence in the so-called Pale of Settlement, which consisted of the 15 westernmost provinces of Russia and the 10 provinces of Poland then under Russian control. Often associated in the popular mind with political radicalism and turmoil, Jews were the target of increased repression following the assassination of Russia's ruler, Czar Alexander II, in 1881. *Pogroms* (government-sanctioned attacks on Jewish settlements) resulted in the death of hundreds of Russian Jews and stimulated thousands more to emigrate. In 1882 about 13,000 arrived in the United States, more than in the entire previous decade. In the 1890s the numbers continued to spiral, and between 1900 and 1914 nearly 1.5 million arrived, with a peak of 152,000 in 1906 alone. Unlike the German Jews, who earlier had spread out across the United States, making cities like Cincinnati and San Francisco major Jewish centers, the Jews from eastern Europe flocked to a few large urban centers in the Midwest and on the Atlantic Coast. By 1920, more than half of all American Jews lived in three cities: New York, Philadelphia, and Chicago.

As was the case with other immigrant groups, the Russian Jews were young, but unlike the others, many were married and nearly half (44 percent) were women. This leads historians to assume that most intended to stay in America, a deduction borne out by statistics. Between 1908 (when the United States first began keeping records of those who left the country) and 1924, only 1 in 20 of the Jewish immigrants returned to Europe. In the earlier years, before official records were kept, the return rate was probably higher. One historian estimated that from 15 to 20 percent of the Russian Jews who came to America between 1800 and 1900 returned home.

A Russian Jew awaits processing at the immigration station on Ellis Island in 1900. A renewed wave of anti-Semitism in Russia convinced many Jews to emigrate in the final two decades of the 19th century.

This return rate is small compared to other immigrant groups, but it should not be discounted. Historians point out that Jews forced from Europe by violence and discrimination often felt that they had no choice, that they could not go back. The permanent nature of Jewish immigration is often cited as one of its distinguishing characteristics. All this is true, but at least five percent, and at times more, did return, and the sheer volume of Jewish immigration means that a considerable number found life in America not to their liking.

Newspaper reports of the day indicate that Jewish returnees were not uncommon. In 1888, New York City's *Jewish Messenger* noted that "hundreds of dispirited people are as eager to leave the United States as a few years or months ago they were hopeful in reaching it" and were willing to take passage on any ship available, even those designed to carry livestock. In Boston, a newspaper recorded that 75 newly arrived Jewish immigrants had rushed to a steamship office after learning that they could obtain free passage home there.

Sometimes immigrants were coerced into returning. Those immigrants who could not find work and thus threatened to become charges of the community were encouraged, often not so subtly, to return home. How often this return was forced on an immigrant remains unclear, but such incidents were not unknown. Most charity organizations insisted that they left the matter up to the individual, but usually whoever controlled the money was ultimately persuasive. Historian Jonathan Sarna wrote about one man who was told by a Jewish charity organization, "If you cannot succeed here, you had better go back." The United Hebrew Charities (UHC), another organization that helped Jews adjust to their adopted country, sometimes had to arrange and pay for passage for those who wanted to leave. One physician who worked for the UHC calculated that between 1882 and 1889 a total of 7,580 persons received the organization's assistance in order to return home. Other estimates are even higher.

Those Jews familiar with the difficulty of life in America sent word that only the strongest should attempt immigration. In 1881 a Russian group in New York wrote to a sister organization in Paris that the sick and weak should be discouraged, or they would find "prompt action being taken to secure their return to Europe." When objections were raised to this policy of returning Jews to Europe, one physician explained why such measures were necessary: "It must be remembered that as American Israelites we have a duty to the community in which we live, which forbids us to become parties to the infliction of permanent paupers upon our already overburdened city."

Some of the least savory stories concern men sent back aboard cattle ships. One probably scurrilous report maintained that the UHC received five dollars for each

The meanness and want experienced by many immigrants is evident in this late-19th-century photograph of an immigrant woman's kitchen. Finding themselves living a life of poverty amid plenty in America, many of the new immigrants returned to Europe, preferring to endure hardship surrounded by the consolations of family, friends, and home.

Poor Jewish immigrants are provided with free groceries on New York City's Lower East Side during the early days of the 20th century. Some of the Jewish charitable organizations created to relieve poverty encouraged destitute immigrants to return home.

passenger thus returned. Hired to tend the livestock, the men were often misled about their hours and duties. Engaged in New York City to work four hours a day in return for passage to Europe, they found their conditions changed once the ships put out to the sea. Some of the men reported that they were expected to work from 3:30 A.M. straight through until 10:00 P.M. When they objected, they were beaten; and they were given only a little bread, some hot water, and a few potatoes to eat each day.

Those who survived such treatment received a cool welcome in Europe, where they were viewed as empty-pocketed failures. Undesired when they left, they found that few nations were willing to admit them upon their return. In 1910 the government of Prussia, the most powerful kingdom in the German empire, passed regulations concerning the returned Jews. Before entering the country, each was required to show possession of a certain amount of money and a ticket to go elsewhere. In addition, Jews could also be compelled to travel in special trains.

In spite of the available evidence on how repatriates were treated, some Jews continued to go back. One rabbi reportedly said that some Jews immigrated only to make money while others who had meant to stay changed their minds when they had trouble finding steady work.

The return home was not always intended to be permanent. Some Jews made what they thought would be a short trip—to visit aged parents, study, find a wife, or make a show of what they had acquired. Once there, they lingered. Then the condition of the parents worsened or the chosen bride refused to leave; the course of study stretched from one year to many. The familiarities of home exerted a tighter grip, and the return visit became a permanent stay.

Other Jewish immigrants had clearly never intended to stay in America. Success stories were reported, some modest and some not. One man from the Polish city of Bialystok accumulated $20,000 in America and then took it home to start a factory. Another man, who had been a beggar in Russia, boasted that he came to America to earn a dowry for his daughter. After five years, he was pleased to report that he had saved $250, enough to find a fine son-in-law.

For some religious Jews, the difficulty of worshiping in their own way was the primary reason for rejecting America. One man noted how quickly his fellow Jews fell into neglect of the Sabbath and the holy days. He called America "a godless land."

Other Jews were disillusioned by the filth and crowded living conditions they found in American cities and were dismayed at the presence of poverty in the land of plenty. One Russian lamented in a letter written in 1902 to a Jewish newspaper: "Where is the golden land, where are the golden people?" For various reasons, many Jewish immigrants decided that the golden land was the home they had left behind, the golden people their families, friends, and neighbors in the old country. Little could they know that in a matter of decades the Europe they longed for would become an even more inhospitable place, in which to be Jewish marked one not only for oppression but for extermination.

Jewish schoolchildren in Connecticut in 1940 study a map of Palestine, which the Zionist movement had designated as the Jewish homeland. For many years Palestine was the destination of Jewish immigrants. In May 1948, Jews there proclaimed the existence of the independent state of Israel, which many of the world's Jews continue to regard as their homeland.

The Greeks

Before 1890, only a few hundred Greeks entered the United States each year, but by the end of the decade overpopulation and the resulting economic distress, particularly in the countryside, were encouraging mass migration. In 1907, the peak year of Greek immigration, 46,283 Greeks came to America.

The motivation of most of the immigrants was the usual one—the opportunity to earn some money and enjoy a better standard of living. Although starvation was rare in rural Greece at the end of the 19th century, food was scarce. According to an American consul there, a worker could expect only bread and coffee for breakfast, bread and olives for lunch, and the same, with the addition of a few vegetables and some rice, in the evening. Meat was reserved for special holidays.

Word of America's bountiful harvests found receptive listeners in Greece. Eager to rid the country of those whom it could neither feed nor employ, the Greek government encouraged emigration, as did others—steamship agents who wanted to fill ships and labor recruiters who had promised to supply work gangs. Lenders stood to gain by emigration by putting up the passage money in return for the security of a small plot of land in Greece or some other property.

Zealous labor recruiters went to Greece and convinced families to ship their sons off. Promise of a yearly payment of anywhere from $80 to $250 appealed to parents with many mouths to feed. Few knew that once the deal was arranged and their son was far away, he might be required to work as many as 90 hours a week.

With so many inducements to emigrate, it is not surprising that thousands of young Greek men left for America. It has been estimated that by 1910 between 20 and 25 percent of Greece's labor force had set out for the United States. More than 90 percent of the immigrants were men. Flocking to the large cities, especially on the eastern seaboard, the men took jobs in restaurants and

Greek miners pose at the beginning of a day's shift in 1903. These miners were fortunate to have work; poverty and hunger among the peasantry in rural Greece drove many to immigrate to the United States. By 1910 nearly one-fourth of Greece's work force had emigrated.

factories. Those who could not immediately locate jobs on their own turned to labor agents to find them work in distant states such as Kansas and Washington. For very young workers, labor agents provided "false fathers" to get them past immigration officials.

Jobs were plentiful, particularly in comparison with what was available in Greece, and the immigrants were able to earn two or three times what they did at home. Because they were so thrifty, Greek workers were able to send much of what they made back home. In 1913 the Greek minister of national economy credited the economic contributions of the emigrants when he noted that in no other country did remittances constitute such an important part of the economy. One Greek commission concluded that temporary emigrants returned 10 times what the country had spent to raise them.

The Greek devotion to the homeland is evident in the number of immigrants who returned. In absolute numbers (not as a percentage of those who came to America), Greeks ranked fourth in returnees between 1908 and 1931—behind Italians, Poles, and English. Some went back to find wives; others returned to raise their children in Greece. The great majority had never intended to stay.

Many returned to serve their country. In 1912, when war with Turkey seemed imminent, thousands of Greeks in America sought passage home. Newspapers in Athens encouraged all Greeks, old and young, immigrants and their children, to return and fight as volunteers. So many responded that there were not enough ships bound for Greece to carry them, and some would-be soldiers had to sail to other European ports and then proceed by land. So great was the patriotic fever that gripped Greeks residing in America that some had to wait for days in ports, paying their own expenses, until they found passage home. In all, about 40,000 Greek Americans responded to the battle cry.

Some of the returnees found life in Greece less pleasant than anticipated. Neighbors and relatives sought loans and ridiculed the way the repatriates dressed and talked. Those who had changed their grooming habits during their American sojourn were chided for cutting their hair differently and shaving too often. The returnees were labeled with scornful nicknames: *Brooklis* (Brooklynite), *kounesmenos* (shaken one), and *okay boys* were some of the least offensive. Greek officials joined in disparaging their returned countrymen, and a Cretan mayor announced that "few Greek Americans of any account have returned to Greece."

Despite this cold reception, Greeks continued to figure among the largest returning immigrant groups until American laws cut off their unrestricted entry in the 1920s. Theodore Saloutos, a historian who studied the return movement to Greece, concluded that in 1920, a typical year, more than 20,000 Greeks returned to their

homeland. More than half of them had resided in America between 5 and 10 years; another 6,000 had stayed less than that time. Most had come in their teens, Saloutos concluded, and were returning as mature men. Almost all of them took some money back, although the amount varied. Those who had managed to start businesses sometimes managed to accumulate several thousand dollars, whereas others, limited to unskilled labor, could pay little more than their own return passage and that of the family members who accompanied them.

The high rate of Greek repatriation ceased when entry to the United States became more difficult. The immigration quota legislation of the 1920s granted Greeks only a small allotment. Once individual Greeks were forced to wait a long time to emigrate, sometimes even for years, they were more reluctant to return once they finally made it to the United States. Greeks began to show a tendency to immigrate as families, and most intended to stay.

In New York City, a wagon is piled high with the luggage of Greeks eager to return to fight for the homeland during the Balkan Wars, which began in 1912.

ITALIAN BIRDS
OF PASSAGE

Italians have always been among the world's emigrating peoples. Their boot-shaped peninsula gives them 2,000 miles of access to the sea, and travelers from the north of Italy have long made their way over the Alps to France, Germany, Switzerland, and other countries.

Mass immigration to the New World did not begin until the latter half of the 19th century, after the Risorgimento, the period of cultural nationalism and political activity that led to Italy's unification as a nation. Prior to unification, the southern kingdoms of Sicily and Naples had often fallen under foreign domination, but following the Risorgimento political power in unified Italy rested largely in the north, and the oppressed peasantry of the south found their situation little improved. By 1900, Italy's population density was among the highest on the continent, and industrialization and modernization had not made deep inroads in the south, where landless peasants continued to toil for absentee landlords, using the same type of primitive implements that they had worked with for centuries. The peasants tilled soil made all but barren by decades of overuse, and floods and erosion carried off what good earth remained. The little money the peasants earned went to pay taxes imposed by the new national government. Illness, malnutrition, a shortened life span—all the legacies of entrenched poverty characterized life in the south of Italy.

A Magical Land

It is little wonder then that by 1880 Italians, most of them peasants from the south, were emigrating in droves. The talk in the south was of America, a name that took on almost magical connotations of wealth and success. Eventually Italians would come to see that their own land also offered opportunity—they would boast that "America is here"—but in the late 1800s, America still lay more than 4,000 miles west across the Atlantic.

Those Italians who immigrated to America before 1880—their numbers rarely exceeded 1,000 in any one year—generally hailed from the north, from the Ligurian coast or Piedmont. They boasted more education and skills than their countrymen from the south. Perhaps because they were better suited in this way for life in the United States or Canada, the northern Italians immigrated with the intention of staying in America. They brought their families with them, and many settled on the Pacific Coast, not a convenient place from which to return home.

After 1880 the number of Italians seeking to emigrate skyrocketed: There were 11,482 in 1881, 44,359 in 1891, and more than 63,000 by 1899. Ultimately, one person was leaving Italy each year for every hundred who remained, and about 20 percent of those going were headed for the United States. Most were men from the south, uneducated (sometimes illiterate) and unskilled

workers who expected to find work at the construction sites or the docks of America's major cities.

Few of them meant to stay. As Italian observer Leone Carpi noted in 1871: "Thousands of Italians go to search for work abroad, then come back within a year or two bringing with them a small amount of savings along with some bad habits." Another Italian pointed out that his countrymen "carry their mother country in their hearts and return as soon as they have put together a small nest egg." The rate of return was so great that the Italian government soon began to record the number of those returning, just as they recorded the number of those emigrating. Beginning in 1884, the government required that captains of ships entering Italian ports report how many passengers they carried in third class and which countries they had left. The assumption was that conditions in third class were so bad that only returning immigrants would travel that way.

An Italian family in the Sicilian town of Messina camps amid the ruins of its home, which was destroyed by an earthquake. Natural disaster accented the precariousness of life among the rural populace and sent many men to America in search of a better life for their family.

Successful returnees probably chose better accommodations, and some returnees landed first in other countries and then proceeded homeward by train. But in the absence of other information, the number who arrived in third class gives some picture of repatriation. By 1899, almost half of the returnees came from the United States.

Ironically, the fever to emigrate was fed, in part, by those who had already gone and then come back. One young man told how the stories related by the returnees were "as amazing as the tales of Columbus when he returned from his first discovery of America." Another compared the returnees with another legendary Italian adventurer, Marco Polo, in that the money to be earned in the United States seemed as fantastic as the treasures Polo said could be found in China. In America, it was said, workers could earn five times what they had earned in Italy.

Aldobrando Piacenza, the son of a day laborer, listened carefully to the accounts of plenty in America. In his childhood in a poor village in central Italy, he had known only hunger and want, too little food and threadbare clothing, but the men returning from America wore watches on gold chains and seemed to have sacks of money. "I dreamed of the time," he wrote in his unpublished memoirs, "when I could also go to see the Beautiful City and return with a beautiful suit and the watch with the gold chain."

Not all came back in glory. Some returned exhausted and ill. With no words spoken, faces worn and aged by grueling factory work told frightening stories, but many young men were more afraid of becoming like the emaciated peasants who had never left than of any hardships America might hold. In any case, a trip to America was part of growing up, a rite of passage: "You weren't a man," one Italian wrote, "until you'd seen America."

Entire towns in southern Italy lost almost all their young men to emigration. Only old people, young children, and women remained. Stories were often told of mayors in southern Italy who greeted visitors "in the name of all the inhabitants. Half of them are in America and the others are preparing to go."

The Lure of Home

But as thousands of Italians left each year, thousands more returned. In 1908 the United States began compiling its own figures on returns. That year, U.S. officials reported that 166,733 Italians had gone back, most of them spurred by an economic downturn that had left many without work. The numbers in the following years were smaller but hardly insignificant: 83,300 in 1909; 52,323 in 1910; 72,640 in 1911. Then, as tensions in Europe pointed toward war, the numbers grew even higher: 108,388 in 1912; 88,021 in 1913; 84,351 in 1914; and a huge exodus of 96,903 in 1915.

Nine out of 10 returnees were male. October to December was always the peak period of return, indicating that most of the repatriates were workers in largely seasonal trades—construction or agriculture, for example—who were returning home because their work was ended for the year. Three-fourths were between 16 and 45 years of age. Most of the elderly returnees were women, many of them widows.

Although many individuals traveled between Italy and the United States several times, few made the trip each year. Even at a cost of between $10 and $30, the voyage was expensive. The average stay in the United States was five years.

Temporary immigration constituted a delicate problem for the United States and Italy in their relations with each other. Italy was grateful to have the United States as an outlet for its excess population, and the remittances sent back by the immigrants benefited the Italian economy. The United States profited from the sweat and muscle of the young men Italy sent over, but a large segment of its population believed that dollars earned in the United States should stay there. Many Americans felt that the temporary immigrants were taking advantage of the United States, that they came only to earn money without making any commitment of loyalty to the nation that afforded them such an opportunity. Some Italians conceded the truth of the American complaints. One Italian official concluded that the temporary immigrants were truly "birds of passage who hardly ever spend money in America and hate everything which is American except the gold that takes them away." Keenly aware of American resentments, the Italian Parliament formed an Emigration Commission in 1901 to monitor the situation and keep abreast of American attitudes.

A few of the temporary immigrants had no choice but to return, and for the most part Americans were glad to see these unfortunate Italians go. Very poor, sick, or orphaned Italians could appeal to consulates in America for passage home at a nominal charge. Shipping companies were required to provide indigent immigrants with cheap return trips, the exact number to be based on the total number of passengers the ship had carried over. About five percent of the returnees used this option to get home.

The Italian government understood that men who left their family in Italy to go work in America would send money home, but that remittances would stop when families were united across the Atlantic. Accordingly, one of the functions of the Emigration Commission was to encourage temporary emigration. In addition to regulating the cost of shipping and the sanitary conditions, food, and medical attention on board, the commission also assigned to the Bank of Naples the job of transmitting funds from the workers to their families. Men who never learned English and were not comfortable writing had difficulty finding ways to get money to the old country. They used postal money orders, relied on friends who were going, or sent their own envelopes through the mail. The Bank of Naples, where Italian was spoken, made the process easier.

The total amount of money returned to Italy as remittances can never be known. The Emigration Commission reported that remittances from the United States totaled more than $3 million in 1903, a figure that had tripled by 1911. Through thrift and self-denial, Italian immigrant workers in the United States were often able to save half of what they earned. Of course, at $1.50 a day (the typical wage for a laborer at that time), savings accumulated slowly, but typically a returning laborer brought home with him between $250 and $1,000. An exceptionally successful repatriate could bring as much as $2,000.

The influx of remittance money into Italy had mixed results for the Italian economy. Individual families profited, of course. One woman, whose father worked in Boston and New York while his wife and three daughters lived outside Naples, remembered how the grocer always gave them credit. "I would go down to buy things," she recalled, "and when it came time to pay, the grocer would ask 'Is your father still in America?' I would say 'yes' and then the grocer put everything on our bill. At the end of the month, when money arrived

Because the U.S. and Italian governments had a common interest in monitoring immigration, they sometimes cooperated with one another on immigration questions. These Italian fugitives from military service in the homeland were shipped back to Italy by the United States.

from my father, we would settle up. With a father in America, we always had credit."

Remittance money also went toward investments in land and businesses. Property bought with dollars earned in America could support a family for years. One man who worked in New York from 1906 to 1912 lived 60 years after returning, and he could not have purchased a better pension than the income offered by the land bought with his American dollars. At age 97, he could point down the road to the homes of others who had similarly benefited and say, "America bought most of these houses." But prices rose when remittances were high, and some employers complained that men who could acquire their own land were unwilling to work for others. Landowners, no longer able to find cheap labor, claimed that they had no other choice but to sell their holdings.

The returnees brought other unwelcome changes as well. Exposed to new illnesses abroad, the men returned sick, often with tuberculosis. Some had started drinking excessively, and others had acquired a taste for gambling. Many reportedly carried knives. One Italian official complained: "Alcoholism, a previously unknown habit among our rural population, is already beginning to spread in the areas of great emigration."

Sometimes it was simply the men's attitude that had changed, often for the worse, according to their compatriots. One Italian senator told his colleagues: "These men return from abroad, unable to work in the fields. They make fun of this country. They cannot get used to the modest life here. They return three or four times to America where they end up Americanized or else stay in Italy where they are of little use as citizens."

Opinion was unanimous on the effect of temporary emigration on family life. Whatever the economic benefits of having a father working in America, the family suffered. One official blamed emigration for the "increasing number of cases of adultery, of illegitimate births, of abortions, of infanticides and of a series of crimes that are linked to the weakening of the family structure."

But for all the problems it engendered, temporary emigration served Italy well. It was far better for young men to go to work in America and send money home than to remain idle and unproductive in Italy, where they would form a potential source of political and social unrest. Temporary emigration was a more acceptable solution to Italy's economic woes than permanent emigration, which left, one Italian official noted, "a bloody wound."

For these reasons, the official government policy was to welcome the returnees. Reduced train fares were offered from port cities to cities and towns in the interior. Even those who had become American citizens were welcomed, and bulletins reminded all who wanted to hear that "Italians who go to search for work in the United States, if they return, the mother country will never refuse to recognize them as her sons." Official pronouncements from the government praised temporary immigration. The Foreign Minister Pittoni warned: "It would be terrible if this safety valve did not exist, this possibility of finding work elsewhere." Italian senator Eduardo Pantiano completed the idea: "The great current of returning emigrants represents an economic force of the first order for us. It will be an enormous benefit for us if we can increase this flow of force in and out of our country."

Forced by circumstance into a situation where they often felt they had little choice but to emigrate, the men who traveled between America and Italy were often less enthusiastic than the statesmen for whom emigration served a political purpose. "Work" or "money" were the succinct answers usually given by immigrants when asked why they left the homeland. An even more compelling reason—family—was what most often brought them back.

For many of the temporary immigrants, their years in America constituted a complex experience, the effects of

The establishment of local branches of Italian banks in the United States made it easier for temporary immigrants to send remittances back home to their family.

which were still being felt years afterward. One Sicilian, whose father worked for five years in Brooklyn and then returned to Italy, explained: "My father went as a young man, eager to find a better life than he had here. Instead he found a city full of noise and chaos so he came back to Agrigento. He never encouraged any of his sons to emigrate because he knew that the better life was here in Sicily."

But the father's move affected his family in several ways. He encouraged his children to continue their schooling—something that few unskilled workers in Italy talked about—and enrolled himself in classes to become a mechanic. Despite his negative impressions of America, he was proud of the English he had learned in New York and offered friendly greetings to American soldiers who landed in Sicily during World War II— more than 30 years after he had left America. As the years passed, this Sicilian tended to forget the bad parts of his American stay and to remember the good. His son, who heard his father reminisce often, explained after the father's death: "Eventually he forgot his disappointments and remembered only the extravagances of the experience. Perhaps it was there that he could buy his first suit of clothes. He always spoke of America as a very big and different place, much as one might speak of a noisy festival that one has attended in order to boast of being present rather than for any enjoyment of the event itself."

The immigrants who returned often suffered from divided loyalties. Decades after returning to Italy, the men continued to reminisce about the pleasures of America. Some remembered the abundant water— especially welcome to those who came from parts of Italy where drought was common. Others fondly recalled the relative absence of social distinctions. "Here in Italy," one said, "if I go into an office or a shop, it's Doctor or Professor. But in America, everybody is Mister." Impressed by the efficiency and material wealth of America, they yet remained committed to the more relaxed way of life in Italy. But after their return, many felt out of place in the Italian villages where they had grown up. Their American experiences set them apart from those who had never left, and they knew they were accused of "putting on airs." Neither fully American nor completely Italian, they had one foot in each country. "In Italy, they call me an American," many would say, "but in America, they know immediately that I am Italian."

By the second decade of the 20th century, sentiment was building to end the influx of foreigners to the United States. The men behind bars are illegal aliens seized in a roundup in New York City in 1917.

CLOSING THE DOOR

By the 1920s, many Americans were loudly demanding that Congress close the open door that the United States had long offered to the world. The new immigrants from southern and eastern Europe had never been as well received as their predecessors from the Old World. Racial and religious prejudice accounted for some of the hostility with which they were met. In 1910, for example, a congressional committee issued a 42-volume report that concluded, purportedly on the basis of scientific evidence, that the new immigrants were racially inferior to older American stock and could never successfully adopt the American way of life. Such "scientific" conclusions were, of course, nonsense, yet they reflected popular opinion. Fear and ignorance underlay America's xenophobia—misconceptions about the unknown and strange ways of the newcomers, trepidation that foreigners would take American jobs, and terror that the sheer number of new arrivals would enable them to impose their own language, religion, and way of life on a soon-to-be minority of Americans. Such sentiment was articulated by Senator Albert Johnson of Washington, who stated that Americans had seen "patent and plain, the encroachments of the foreign-born flood upon their own lives. They have come to realize that such a flood, affecting as it does every individual of whatever race or origin, cannot fail likewise to affect the institutions which have made and preserved American liberties. It is no wonder, therefore, that the myth of the melting pot has been discredited. It is no wonder that Americans everywhere are insisting that their land no longer shall offer free and unrestricted asylum to the rest of the world. . . . The day of unalloyed welcome to all peoples, the day of indiscriminate acceptance of all races, has definitely ended."

Temporary immigrants figured prominently in the debate over the foreign influx. Because they did not intend to remain permanently in the United States, temporary immigrants rarely bothered to obtain U.S. citizenship, and Americans who believed that the new immigrants were unwilling to assimilate cited this tendency to bolster their anti-immigration arguments. Americans disliked competing with temporary as well as permanent immigrants for jobs, and labor unions resented the willingness of the new immigrants, including the birds of passage, to work for low wages, which often undercut their efforts to organize on behalf of their members. The temporary immigrants' practice of saving money to take with them upon their return to the homeland aroused much animosity. The inscription on the Statue of Liberty in New York harbor urged Europe to surrender "your tired, your poor, your huddled masses yearning to breathe free," but some nativist Americans believed the temporary immigrants yearned not for freedom but only for the opportunity to return home with a satchel full of dollars. According to such reasoning, this exodus of U.S. money represented an abuse of American hospitality.

The discourse over temporary immigration took on added urgency because of the increased frequency of the

practice. In 1908, the first year for which such records were kept, more than 395,000 former immigrants left the United States. The great majority were eastern and southern Europeans. Nearly 167,000 were Italians. Another 130,000 reported that they were going to live in the Dual Monarchy of Austria-Hungary, which also exerted political control over some of the Slavic regions that today are part of Yugoslavia. Other popular destinations were Russia (37,777) and Greece (6,131). Of the nations of northern and western Europe, the home nations of the old immigrants, only Germany was the destination of a significant number of returnees.

A congressional study determined that many of those who left returned again at a later date. It was not unusual for some individuals to make several trips back and forth in the course of a lifetime.

Economists pointed out that the temporary immigrants were actually a boon to workers in that their

An antinativist cartoon of the 1890s. The caption reads "They would close to the newcomer the bridge that carried them and their fathers over." Portrayed as wealthy members of the American establishment (but each himself the descendant of humbler immigrant ancestors, pictured as shadows behind them) are the supporters of exclusionary immigration legislation, who seek to deny entry to a contemporary would-be immigrant.

Nativists often criticized immigrants for purveying "subversive" and "un-American" political ideology, such as communism. The immigrants in this photo are awaiting deportation at Ellis Island after being arrested as "Reds" in 1920.

presence as a source of cheap labor encouraged expansion, which resulted in more jobs for everyone. In many cases as well, immigrants took jobs that Americans were unwilling to fill, either because the pay was too low, the hours too long, the work too dangerous, or a combination of the three.

But the beliefs of nativist Americans remained unaffected by economists' assessments. They saw only men who spoke foreign tongues and practiced alien ways, concerned only with trying to survive on as little as possible so as to be able to take a large chunk of their earnings with them when they left. Living in male enclaves without the "civilizing" influence of their families, the workers were accused of drunkenness, brawling, filthiness, superstitious religious practices, whoremongering, and other forms of deviant or criminal behavior. Senator Henry Cabot Lodge of Massachusetts, lashing out at the birds of passage, found them little better than animals: "They live in miserable sheds like beasts; the food they eat is so meager, scant, un-wholesome, and revolting that it would nauseate an American workman and he would find it difficult to sustain life upon it."

Congress Acts

Different solutions were advanced for solving the problem of the temporary immigrants. One con-gressman suggested barring all who retained a residence in a foreign country. According to this plan, anyone wanting to work in America would have to show that he had permanently cut his ties to the homeland. But such a measure would have been dif-ficult, if not impossible, to enforce, so another solution was needed—one specifically tailored to exclude im-migrants from countries that had high return rates.

A literacy requirement seemed the perfect answer. Adults would be tested on arrival in American ports. Those who could not read 40 words of some language or dialect would not be permitted to enter. The proposal was aimed specifically at the uneducated laborers and peasants from southern and eastern Europe. As one professor who worked with the American Immigration Commission pointed out, such a law would exclude "the laborers from southern Italy and Austria-Hungary of the type that ought to be excluded, especially the single man who comes here to stay only temporarily." The literacy requirement was a blatant attack on temporary im-migrants, most of whom came from countries where schooling was poor or unavailable.

The literacy requirement had a long legislative his-tory. It was first sponsored in Congress in 1896 by Henry Cabot Lodge. Congress ultimately approved the measure, but President Grover Cleveland did not and vetoed it. Further attempts to pass the literacy require-ment were made in 1898, 1902, and 1906, but they were defeated by the Democrats, who drew much of their support from immigrants and their descendants. Presidents William Howard Taft and Woodrow Wilson administered vetoes to literacy measures sent up by Congress in 1913 and 1915. In 1917, Congress overrode Wilson's veto, and the literacy requirement became part of the Immigration Law of that year.

During three decades of debate, the literacy law had gained many supporters. The Immigration Restriction League, a Boston-based group, had been pushing the idea since the 1890s. One of the league's bulletins explained: "Taking the world as it is, we find, on a broad view, that the illiterate races and especially the illiterate individuals of those races, are the ones who are undesirable, not merely for their illiteracy but for other reasons." The American Federation of Labor also supported the literacy test requirement, as did the Farmers' Educational and Cooperative Union, the National Grange, and the Farmers' National Congress.

Opponents of the literacy law pointed out that it would apply an unfair test to prospective newcomers. In his veto message in 1915, Woodrow Wilson detected an ironic consequence that would ensue should the measure be adopted: "Those who are seeking opportunity are not to be admitted unless they have already had one of the chief opportunities they seek, the opportunity of education."

Countries that supplied large numbers of immigrants watched carefully while Americans debated the literacy law. In 1902, Italian official Luigi Bodio recommended that his government establish schools in southern Italy so that prospective emigrants could attend classes after work or on holidays and make up for the basic schooling they had not received as children. Action was delayed when it became apparent that the literacy requirement would not immediately become law, but in 1914 the Italian government acted to open centers in order to "rapidly prepare emigrants to surmount the obstacles resulting from illiteracy."

Then World War I intervened, and immigration from Europe, including Italy, dropped to a fraction of its

former size. Men were needed at home to fight, and travel across the Atlantic was dangerous. The number of Europeans who arrived in the United States dropped abruptly, from more than 1 million in 1914 to fewer than 200,000 in 1915. By 1918 that figure had dwindled to 31,000. The wartime immigrants included almost no birds of passage.

When immigration resumed on a large scale, the literacy law had little impact. Italy, for example, carefully monitored American practices and policies and administered its own reading test to emigrants before they

A cartoon from the early 20th century portrays a convivial Uncle Sam welcoming the representatives of many immigrant groups to the national feast, but there was already strong public sentiment to close America's open door.

left. Those who failed were counseled to try countries other than the United States. Only a few thousand Italians actually arrived in the United States and failed the test—319 in 1917, 1,598 in 1918, and 1,456 in 1919.

Following the conclusion of World War I, Europeans were again able to think about immigrating. By 1921, three years after the war's end, 650,000 Europeans immigrated to the United States. One-third of that number left that same year. Obviously, the literacy requirement had failed to stop temporary immigration.

In 1921 and again in 1924, the U.S. Congress passed comprehensive immigration legislation. Both acts were based on the concept of establishing quotas for the number of immigrants granted entry from specific countries. The Quota Act of 1921 set the limit for each admissible nationality at three percent of the foreign-born population of that nationality as recorded in the U.S. Census of 1910. The limits placed on immigrants from southern and eastern Europe reduced the maximum admitted from each nation there to less than one-fourth of the number admitted prior to World War I.

Even this measure failed to fully pacify nativist Americans. Cosponsored by Senator Johnson, the Immigration Act of 1924 imposed even more stringent quotas. The maximum total of immigrants admitted in a year was set at 165,000, to be apportioned on the basis of a ceiling for each individual nation of 2 percent of the foreign born of that nationality as recorded in the 1890 census. Because the majority of the new immigrants had arrived after 1890, the nations of eastern and southern Europe were particularly hard hit by the new legislation. In 1927 the quota method was replaced by a national origins criterion that was equally restrictive regarding the new immigrants. The new quotas for Italians, Greeks, and Slavs amounted to a mere three percent of their annual immigration average before World War I.

The Immigration Act of 1924 all but halted mass immigration from southern and eastern Europe. Frequent back-and-forth travel broken by lengthy sojourns in order to work became a practical impossibility, and men and women who had waited for months and even years to obtain a visa to immigrate to the United States were not likely to return home after only a short stay. The flights of the birds of passage had come to an end.

The closing of America's open door gave rise to a new problem—illegal immigration—as America's border with Mexico proved much more difficult to patrol than did its traditional ports of entry. These illegal aliens are being deported from southern California in November 1926.

REPATRIATION
IN THE
MODERN ERA

The two immigration acts of the early 1920s resulted in profound alterations in the pattern of immigration to the United States, but changes in U.S. law were not the only factors affecting immigration. Many nations, Italy and the Soviet Union among them, acted to restrict the emigration of their people at about the same time the United States amended its policies. Economic conditions—traditionally a great stimulus for immigration—played their role. In the 1930s, the Great Depression wreaked havoc on the world's economy. Few nations escaped its consequences, but the United States suffered particularly hard. The depression shattered the U.S. economy and left millions of Americans jobless. With city dwellers queued up on breadlines and much of the rural population on the move in search of work, the United States lost its appeal to the impoverished of the rest of the world. The outbreak of World War II in 1939 further interrupted civilian travel across both the Atlantic and the Pacific. In 1943, the low point of immigration to the United States, only about 24,000 immigrants entered. Nearly half of those came from Canada.

Repatriation dropped, too, although exact numbers are not available. Aliens leaving the United States in the 1930s and 1940s were often classified with departing tourists or business travelers. Those immigrants who had obtained U.S. citizenship were recorded as Americans when they left. But nothing indicates that immigrants stopped returning home, and two different streams of repatriation were evident between 1924, the year of the second quota act, and 1965, when U.S. immigration legislation was revised again. The first group of immigrants returned out of choice; the second had return thrust upon them.

European Pensioners

Retirees, the greatest number from Greece and Italy, were heavily represented among the repatriates. Having lived and worked in the United States for years, these individuals—once work no longer dictated where they made their residence—preferred to return to the homeland towns where they had spent their earlier years. During the 1930s and 1940s only a small number returned home; but the numbers swelled in the first decades after World War II as the dollar grew in strength and the retirees realized that their U.S. Social Security checks would enable them to live much better in the homeland than they could in the United States.

In 1962, Giovannie Petrucci, an Italian musician, and his wife, a retired nurse, departed the United States to reside in the small town south of Rome where he had been born. On the income from two very modest pensions, they were able to live almost in luxury, employing a full-time maid to cook and clean for them. With its marble floors and large terraces, their house marked them as among the most prosperous residents of the town. Although they missed certain aspects of life in the United States, both well understood that their American dollars would have bought much less there.

"Of course I miss my friends," Petrucci said. "I liked living in Detroit. But here I have good air, good food. Living is more relaxed. And we don't have to worry about money." During his stay in the United States, the musician had enjoyed no small measure of success, and he had become an American citizen, had married an American woman, and had even been invited to the White House by Eleanor Roosevelt. But the pull of the homeland remained strong, and he continued to define the good life as that lived in a little hill town in Italy.

For other Italians, the decision to return was more difficult. Children and grandchildren born in America did not understand the attraction of the old country, and they made it clear that the longest stay they planned in Italy was a summer vacation. Spouses sometimes disagreed on the issue, with one drawn to the familiar town where relatives still lived while the other insisted on staying close to American friends.

Those who had returned home sometimes discouraged others from following. They talked about how hard it was to adjust to what was in effect a virtually unknown way of life, for home might have changed greatly during the prospective returnee's absence. For many of the retirees, America was now the familiar and the homeland the new. It was not unusual for returnees to lament the advantages of life in America that they had surrendered, such as first-rate banking, transportation, and educational systems.

Greek Retirees

The phenomenon of returnees whose golden years were made easier by American pensions was even more well known in Greece. In the 1960s whole villages in Greece looked to the United States for income, and Skoura, fewer than 10 miles from Sparta, was described as "a suburb of New York." This town of 500 people was hardly unique in relying on American dollars. Thousands of Greeks received monthly pensions or Social Security payments, but the concentration in Skoura gained special attention. Each month, a Sparta bank sent a truck loaded with cash to convert the checks into Greek currency.

People from Skoura and elsewhere in Greece emigrated in the early 1950s because of a combination of low wages, lack of jobs, and political instability. Often a son left first and helped a brother or sister immigrate once he had found work, usually in a restaurant or factory. Many of the immigrants expected to return to Skoura as soon as they had saved a certain amount of money or paid off an old debt. One man, after working in a New Jersey restaurant for 12 years, retired to Skoura in the 1960s with $10,000. Another brought no nest egg, but his years of employment in a Connecticut hotel had qualified him for monthly Social Security checks. His $273 per month went much farther in Skoura than in Connecticut, but economics was not his sole reason for returning. He missed his 12 grandchildren, all of whom continued to live in Connecticut, but his wife, who had never learned English, "had no one to talk to there." With its high concentration of elderly, Skoura resembled a retirement community. "It's an old age home here," one resident said, "with green dollars." Money brought back by the returnees was supplemented by sums sent by children still working in America. In addition to food, clothing, and medical care, the dollars bought land and renovated houses. One woman from Skoura barely exaggerated when she said, "We live from America."

Mexicans

Mexicans who returned home between 1924 and 1965 told entirely different stories, but the history of their nation's relationship with its northern neighbor had been quite unlike that of other countries supplying

immigrants. Before the 2,000-mile-long boundary between Mexico and the United States was established in the 1840s, men and women moved freely throughout the region, and they continued to do so after the line was drawn.

Indeed, much of the southwestern region of the United States once belonged to Mexico. Between 1845 and 1854, the United States gained by war and purchase nearly half of Mexico's territory, including some or all of what later became the states of Arizona, California, Colorado, Nevada, New Mexico, Texas, Utah, and Wyoming. Along with the descendants of the original Spanish settlers, the approximately 80,000 Mexicans then living in the region helped give it a permanent Hispanic flavor. The area's architecture and food continued to reflect their influence, and Spanish was widely spoken.

Before 1900 only a few hundred Mexicans reportedly entered the United States as immigrants. Adventurers from Mexico's Sonora region, just south of California, went north during the gold rush of the late 1840s, and other parts of northern Mexico supplied workers for American cattlemen and cotton growers. Other

In 1926, U.S. border patrol officers present arms at the Rio Grande, which for much of its length constitutes the border between Mexico and Texas. In the modern era, most immigration to the United States has come from the south—Mexico and Central and South America—and from Asia.

Mexicans entered the United States uncounted, but the rate of immigration remained low.

Changes in Mexico set the stage for an increased migration northward after 1900. Mines and factories in northern Mexico had begun to draw workers from regions farther south. After uprooting themselves and acquiring the skills needed to obtain new jobs, some *campesinos* (peasants) chose to continue on to what they hoped would be even better opportunities in the United States. The construction of the Mexican railroad made travel easier. Hired hands who worked the fields of small landowners frequently found themselves without jobs when the expanding *haciendas* (plantations) took over more of the land. Political unrest and instability, marked by periods of violence and repression, added to the exodus.

During the same decades, several kinds of jobs suitable for unskilled laborers were opening up in the United States. On the farms, the need for seasonal laborers was high. Railroads, mines, and factories all needed workers, especially after the United States entered World War I in 1917.

A Mexican migrant worker and his family in their shack in Minnesota in 1937. Once valued as an important source of agricultural labor, Mexicans were excoriated as unwelcome competition for American jobs during the depression years of the 1930s.

By the 1920s immigration from Mexico had reached unprecedented heights. Nearly 500,000 Mexicans—11 percent of the total legal immigration—entered the United States during that decade. The quota laws that shut out many European groups did not apply to Mexicans, who moved to fill the gap. In addition to those who came legally, with permanent visas in hand, others entered informally and did not take the time to fill out the necessary papers. Some were ignorant of the laws; other wanted to avoid paying the head tax or the visa charges.

Although employers welcomed the cheap labor Mexicans provided, the immigrants were often the targets of prejudice and discrimination and incurred the wrath of nativist Americans.

The Border Patrol was organized under the U.S. Bureau of Immigration in 1924, and American officials started requiring that Mexicans pass the literacy test. Although some Mexicans had been educated, many could not read the 40 words "in some language or dialect" required for entry. Those who failed were turned away, even though the work they had planned to do did not require reading or writing.

The Great Depression further hardened the animosity felt toward Mexican Americans. White Americans who were displaced from their farms by economic hardship and natural disaster claimed many of the jobs in the fields formerly held by Mexicans. For example, in California prior to the depression, fewer than 20 percent of the migrant farm workers had been white. During the depression, as California's population was swelled by refugees from the dust bowl (the prairie states of the Midwest, where much of the arable topsoil had been blown off by winds), that figure rose to 85 percent. Many of those they replaced were Mexicans. Once seen as a valuable labor force, Mexicans were now despised as likely public burdens.

Reflecting popular opinion, the U.S. government instituted a repatriation program. Free train rides back to

Mexico were offered to those willing to return; those who could not prove that they were legal residents were threatened with deportation. In all, some 500,000 Mexicans returned home during the Great Depression.

When the military's need for manpower left the United States with a diminished labor force during World War II, the government again encouraged Mexicans to come north. Under the *bracero* (hired hand) program, which lasted, with interruption, from 1942 to 1964, the government issued temporary visas to Mexican workers. By 1947, an estimated 200,000 Mexicans had participated in the program, nearly half of them in California. In 1960, one in four seasonal agricultural workers in the United States was Mexican.

Other Mexicans worked as cutters and sewers in the clothing industry. One manufacturer, operating in Los Angeles in the 1960s, explained, "The Mexicans come over with coyotes [individuals who make their living by guiding immigrants over the border] and they come to work with me. So what if one day an immigration official finds them and sends them back? Within two days, they will be back in my shop."

He paused, as though to emphasize his point, and then continued: "And if they don't make it back on their own, I will go down and get them. My factory depends on their labor." He did not have to mention how little he paid them—that was understood. Nor did he have to mention what would happen to them when neither he nor another employer needed them—they would simply return home and wait until they were needed again.

Immigration and Return after 1965

The pattern of immigration to the United States changed dramatically after 1965, in part because of new legislation. The Hart-Celler Act of that year abolished the old quotas and removed barriers to immigration from Asia. After 1965 admission was granted on the basis of a preference system that rewarded those with

President Lyndon Johnson signs the Hart-Celler Act into law in the shadow of the Statue of Liberty on October 3, 1965. The act was the first large-scale revision of U.S. immigration law in more than 40 years.

close relatives already in the United States and those who possessed job skills needed by American employers.

Enormous changes in transportation and communication also combined to affect immigration. Air travel reduced ocean voyages of several days' duration to a matter of hours. By 1970, 10 passengers traveled by air to the United States for every 1 who came by sea. At the same time, improved telephone communication and faster mail service tied continents together so that separations from family and friends seemed less ominous. The mass media also played a role. Television, movies, magazines, and newspapers brought images of American life to hitherto isolated regions of the world. American products such as soft drinks and blue jeans invaded world markets, and Levis and Coca-Cola became as well known as symbols of America as cowboys and Indians had been in an earlier generation.

The result was a shift in the place of origin of immigrants to the United States. Where once the word

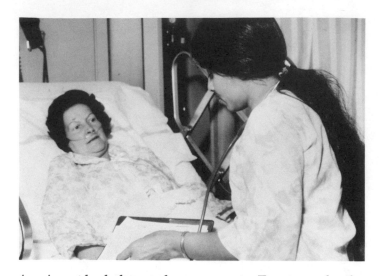

A doctor from India attends to a patient in a New York City hospital. The Hart-Celler Act gives preference to immigrants who possess skills that are in need in the United States. Over the past two decades many doctors and nurses have been admitted under its provisions to help alleviate a shortage of skilled medical professionals.

immigrant had almost always meant a European, by the late 1960s Europe was supplying only one-third of America's immigrants. The largest numbers now came from Asia, Central America, and the Caribbean. In the mid-1970s, China, Korea, and the Philippines were among the five nations that sent the most immigrants to the United States. Other nations that sent large numbers of immigrants to the United States after 1965 include Vietnam, Cambodia, Guatemala, El Salvador, Nicaragua, Mexico, and Jamaica. Although the countries of origin had changed, the immigrants had many of the same reasons for leaving the homeland as had their predecessors years earlier. Political oppression and lack of economic opportunity continued to drive people to seek a better life for themselves and their families in the United States and Canada.

Rate of Return

The exact number of these newest immigrants who have gone back home is unknown, but it is likely that a good percentage do return. As was true of the immigrants from southern and eastern Europe, many make several journeys back and forth. In fact, the relative ease of air travel has probably increased the prevalence of such temporary immigration. For example, the short and cheap flights between the United States and the islands of the Caribbean make some immigrants virtual commuters between two countries. Although they work in the United States, they make trips back so often and maintain such close contact with relatives and friends in their homeland that they seem to be "working away from home" rather than living abroad. A young camera salesman, on a flight to Barbados, explains: "I go back every year—at least. Sometimes I go twice a year. When I have enough money, I will go back to stay." Many of those who reside in the United States on a more permanent basis intend to return permanently to their homeland once the conditions that drove them to emigrate—most notably political violence and repression—have changed. In considering modern repatriation, it should also be noted that an extremely large percentage of today's immigrants, particularly those from Mexico and Central America, enter the United States illegally. Those im-

Not all immigrants who return home do so voluntarily. The anguish of these young illegal immigrants from El Salvador upon learning that they are being deported to their embattled homeland is evident.

migrants, of course, do not enjoy the same freedom of movement as their more fortunate contemporaries.

A New Kind of Immigrant

For the most part, the immigrants who have entered the United States legally since 1965 have been educated professionals, because the Hart-Celler Act gives preference to those individuals. For example, a higher percentage than might otherwise have been expected have been doctors and nurses; the United States has suffered from a shortage of both over the past 20 years. Another distinguishing characteristic of modern immigration has been the large number of women who have immigrated. Traditionally, the great majority of immigrants had been men, but in the 1960s that began to change. Many of the usual opportunities available to immigrant men, such as construction or mine work, were no longer available because of unionization and other changes. Immigrant women now claimed the jobs at the low end of the economic scale—domestic service, work in nonunion clothing sweatshops—that were available to new, often undocumented, arrivals in the United States.

Historically, the presence of large numbers of women among an immigrant group had been seen as an indication that the immigrants in question intended to make their stay a permanent one, but in the 1990s, with immigrant women much more likely to be wage earners and heads of households, this is no longer necessarily true. Where once immigration officials might have denied entrance to a woman traveling alone unless she could offer documentation that she had a male relative in the United States who would look after her, women now immigrate in search of the same opportunities as did male immigrants before them. And it is women who must decide between the lure of the homeland and whatever new life they have made for themselves.

A Central American woman on her way to work in Washington, D.C. More women than ever before are filling the sort of unskilled, low-paying jobs traditionally available to immigrants.

The story of Rosalyn Morris is in many ways representative. Morris came to the United States in 1968 from Jamaica, not Europe, and arrived alone, not with or to join her husband. But her recollections of what made her want to come to America could have been uttered by an immigrant from any generation or country of origin: "I always dreamed that I would come to America. When I was a little girl, I remember people coming back from the United States. They looked so nice. They dressed so nice

Some of the student leaders in the antigovernment protests that rocked China in the spring of 1989 were immigrants who had returned home. That the United States is still seen as a symbol of freedom and democracy is evident by the quotation in English above, first spoken by the American patriot Patrick Henry, which appeared on Democracy Wall in Beijing during the demonstrations.

and talked so nice. When you are not here, you would give your life to come."

Her willingness to sacrifice in order to realize her dream was a characteristic she shared with immigrants of a different time and place. In the city of Kingston, in Jamaica, she earned five dollars a week, hardly enough to make it to the United States. Then she heard of a scheme that involved New York housewives, Jamaican lawyers, and women like herself. In return for her promise to work one year for a New York family, she received a free trip, room and board, and $55 a week. At the end of her term of service, she was free to work out her own arrangements.

Thousands of Jamaican women took advantage of this offer. At age 46, Rosalyn Morris was older than most. "I know I came late to America. Most people immigrate when they are young. I tried earlier but it didn't work out." She explained that after her mother died, she had started working—at age 13, for just a few cents a week plus room and board. At age 20, she had her first child; over the next 14 years, she had 4 others. Morris knew that as long as the children were young, she could not immigrate but, she said, "I kept thinking."

Finally, in 1968, she left the children with an aunt (the youngest was 10) and immigrated to New York. Like many an immigrant before her, she struggled to save enough money to have her family rejoin her, which they did over the course of the next 10 years. Morris has resolved for herself the question of return, but for her children, themselves immigrants, it remains open. "I never expected to get rich in America," she said, but her life is far better than anything she had known in Jamaica. She applied for citizenship as soon as she was eligible, but her children did not, and they fully expect to return to Jamaica at some point. One daughter cites the racism prevalent in the United States and insists that she cannot wait until she has finished college and can return to Jamaica to live. The others talk of working too hard and not liking snow.

Rosalyn Morris points out that should her children return to Jamaica, they will do so with college degrees and consequently with opportunities she never had. Her story highlights some of the central dilemmas of the immigrant experience—the struggle between home and opportunity, the complex play of emotion that accompanies the decision to leave behind kin and country in order to strike out for something better. It has been the purpose of this book to illustrate that such conflicts are seldom resolved permanently merely with the decision to immigrate. It is the lesson of history that they will continue to be central to the immigrant experience.

FURTHER READING

Caroli, Betty Boyd. *Italian Repatriation from the United States.* Staten Island, NY: Center for Immigration Studies, 1973.

Catalano, Julie. *The Mexican Americans.* New York: Chelsea House, 1988.

Daley, William. *The Chinese Americans.* New York: Chelsea House, 1987.

Franco, J. Philip. *The Italian Americans.* New York: Chelsea House, 1987.

Jones, Maldwyn Allen. *American Immigration.* Chicago: University of Chicago Press, 1960.

Kessner, Thomas, and Betty Boyd Caroli. *Today's Immigrants: Their Stories.* New York: Oxford University Press, 1981.

McGill, Allyson. *The Swedish Americans.* New York: Chelsea House, 1988.

Miller, Kerby A. *Emigrants and Exiles.* New York: Oxford University Press, 1985.

Monos, Dimitris. *The Greek Americans.* New York: Chelsea House, 1988.

Muggamin, Howard. *The Jewish Americans.* New York: Chelsea House, 1988.

Seller, Maxine. *To Seek America: A History of Ethnic Life in the United States.* Englewood, NJ: Jerome S. Ozer, 1977.

Shepperson, Wilbur S. *Emigration and Disenchantment.* Norman: University of Oklahoma Press, 1965.

Smead, Howard. *The Afro-Americans.* New York: Chelsea House, 1988.

Watts, J. F. *The Irish Americans.* New York: Chelsea House, 1988.

INDEX

PICTURE CREDITS

BETTY BOYD CAROLI is a history professor at Kingsborough Community College. She received a B.A. from Oberlin College, an M.A. from the University of Pennsylvania, and a Ph.D. from New York University and is the author of several books, including *Today's Immigrants: Their Stories* and *Italian Repatriation from the U.S., 1900–1914*.

DANIEL PATRICK MOYNIHAN is the senior United States senator from New York. He is also the only person in American history to serve in the cabinets or subcabinets of four successive presidents—Kennedy, Johnson, Nixon, and Ford. Formerly a professor of government at Harvard University, he has written and edited many books, including *Beyond the Melting Pot, Ethnicity: Theory and Experience* (both with Nathan Glazer), *Loyalties,* and *Family and Nation.*